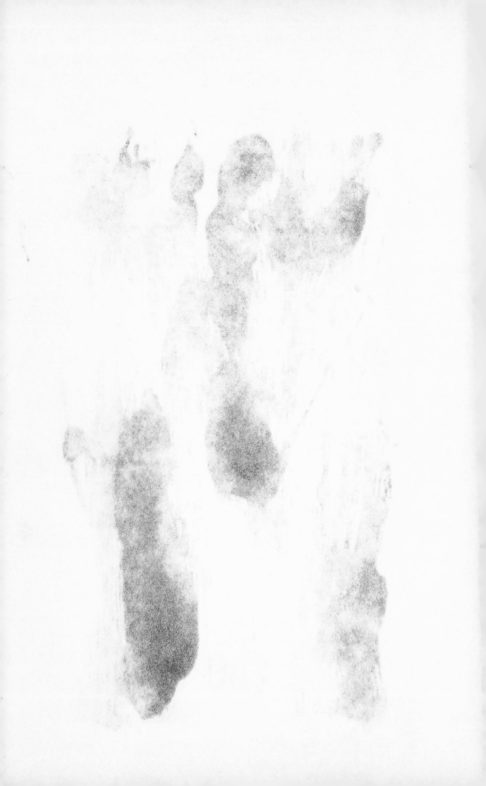

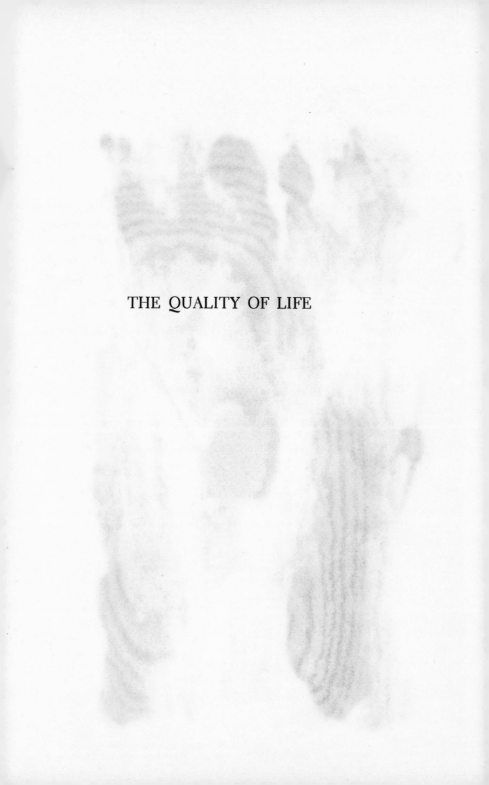

THE QUALITY OF LIFE

THE QUALITY OF LIFE is one of the IMPACT BOOKS, a series designed to bring the modern reader the signifiant achievements of scholars, both Catholic and non-Catholic, in the fields of Scripture, Theology, Philosophy, Mathematics, History, and the Physical and Social Sciences. Among the titles in the series are:

This Good News: An Introduction to the Catholic Theology of the New Testament by Quentin Quesnell, S.J.

Maturing in Christ: St. Paul's Program for Growth in Christ by George T. Montague, S.M.

New Testament Essays by Raymond E. Brown, S.S.

Jesus God and Man by Raymond E. Brown, S.S.

God and Contemporary Man by Robert J. Kreyche

With the Eyes of Faith by Rev. John L. Murphy

Catechetics by Alfred McBride, O.Praem

The God of Exodus by James Plastaras, C.M.

The Biblical Meaning of Man by Dom Wulstan Mork, O.S.B.

The Gospel of Eternal Life by Dominic M. Crossan, O.S.M.

The Word Dwells Among Us by William E. Lynch, C.M.

The Person and the Group by John Thornhill, S.M.

Christ and Original Sin by Peter De Rosa

Jesus in the Synoptic Gospels by William E. Lynch, G.M.

God Our Savior: A Study of the Atonement by Peter De Rosa

An Existential Approach to Theology by G. M. A. Jansen, O.P.

Biblical Theology of the Secular by George T. Montague, S.M.

Changing the Face of the Earth by Patrick Fannon, S.M.

Voices of Convergence by David J. Leary

The Quality of Life

REFLECTIONS ON THE MORAL VALUES OF AMERICAN LAW

CHARLES P. KINDREGAN

PROFESSOR OF LAW, SUFFOLK UNIVERSITY
SCHOOL OF LAW, BOSTON, MASSACHUSETTS

THE BRUCE PUBLISHING COMPANY / MILWAUKEE

FOR TRISH, CHAD, HELEN CHRISTINA,

AND PATRICIA:

MY LIFE.

Library of Congress Catalog Card Number: 69–17321

Copyright © 1969 The Bruce Publishing Company
Made in the United States of America

INTRODUCTION

The law is a moral construct, a mirror of society's values. The relationship between the Judeo-Christian ethic which inspired western morality and Anglo-American law has been discussed by many commentators. This series of reflections centers on those aspects of the law which attempt to shape the quality of human life. From conception to death the law prohibits, condones, and decrees. The essential and customary functions which an individual performs in his lifetime are limited by legal direction, and at the same time they provide the substance upon which courts and law-making bodies base their judgment of what constitutes a good and value-full life.

Law can never be a perfect instrument of social development, but it is the duty of every man in a democracy to help build a humane and moral system of jurisprudence. These reflections are one man's effort to structure some questions on American attempts to improve the quality of life. The reader will quickly become aware of the fact that the author writes both as a lawyer and as one who accepts the tenets of the Judeo-Christian ethic. However, it is not a work of scholarship nor an attempt to provide a blueprint by which men can live their lives. Maurice Blondel once wrote that real history is composed of human life; so also, I suspect, are morals and law. There are theologians and lawyers who will object to my minimization of the abstractions, fictions and propositions of their arts, but I prefer to discuss the problems of human life in terms of man's actual experience to the extent that this can be achieved. There is always a very real danger of a dichotomy between the legal-moral ideal and the problems of man. The cliché thinking which results from abstracting law or morals into a series of rules or propositions is of little or no value.

I have attempted to reduce footnotes to a minimum by providing citations only when quoting an authority or judicial opinion. My purpose is not to write a reference work but to raise some questions about the quality of human life in relation to law and morals.

Thanks are due to my many friends and students who over the years have discussed various aspects of these topics with me, to my colleagues on the faculty at Suffolk University Law School, to Fran Hayes for her help in preparation of the manuscript, and to Dr. William May of The Bruce Publishing Company for his support in this and other writing projects. Most of all I thank my wife Patricia, who makes it all worthwhile.

Charles P. Kindregan
Suffolk University, Boston
October 15, 1968

CONTENTS

CHAPTER I

LIFE CONTROL

In 1925, Carrie Buck was an eighteen-year-old imbecile who was confined in a mental hospital by the state of Virginia. Carrie's mother was also an imbecile. Carrie had borne an illegitimate daughter which in the opinion of a nurse was also imbecilic. The Virginia State Department of Health ordered Carrie to submit to an operation of sterilization for the "best interests of society" since "heredity plays an important part in the transmission of insanity and imbecility." Carrie resisted the order and took her case to the United States Supreme Court. The order of forced sterilization was upheld. Mr. Justice Oliver Wendell Holmes expressed the belief that the state has a right to legislate programs aimed at the elimination of genetically transmissable defects:

> we have seen more than once that the public welfare may call upon the best citizens for their lives. It would be strange if it could not call upon those who already sap the strength of the state for these lesser sacrifices, often felt not to be such by those concerned, in order to prevent our being swamped with incompetence. It is better for all the world, if instead of waiting to execute degenerate offspring for crime, or to let them starve for their imbecility, society can prevent those who are manifestly unfit from continuing their kind . . . (T)hree generations of imbeciles are enough.[1]

If the state can, through legislation, require a person to give up his power of reproduction, how far can it legally and

---

[1] Bell v. Buck 274 U.S. 200 (1925).

morally go in requiring its citizens to submit to techniques of conception control which are aimed at producing superior human beings? The question may startle some, but in recent years a growing number of voices has proposed that there must be control of the process of genetic selection. The geneticist Herman Muller has argued convincingly that deliberate alterations of the principles governing genetic selection are needed if the human species is to survive. Otherwise, Muller believes the decline and extinction of the race is inevitable, because technological culture unifies the race and thereby minimizes the opportunities for human development which multiplicity presents. Furthermore, from a genetic point of view, the race is undergoing a decline as a result of increased merging of genetic combinations. To these factors, Muller adds the opinion that social developments frequently encourage the preservation or even proliferation of characteristics which are harmful to the race. These conditions require, argues Muller, some form of planned conscious control over human reproduction. Such control would aim both at preserving desirable genetic characteristics which have evolved in man and developing desirable traits in future generations.

Eugenics and Controlled Qualitative Improvement of the Race

The belief that the state can take measures which will improve the quality of the race is an ancient one. Plato proposed that "the best of each sex" should be encouraged to unite themselves to "the best of the other sex" as often as possible in order to make "the people of the highest quality." However, it was not until the nineteenth century that concrete legislation was advocated for the purpose of improving man's genetic stock. In 1883 an Englishman, Sir Francis Galton, proposed the creation of a new science to be called eugenics ("wellborn"). Galton believed that racial improvement could be achieved only if families with superior mental and physical histories reproduced in large numbers while propagation by "inferior" families was limited by legal sanctions. Galton's ideas were soon worked into proposals for compulsory sterilization of unfit persons. Among the defects which the early eugenicists felt could be eliminated were tuberculosis, blindness, deafness, pauperism, intoxication, drug addiction, feeblemindedness, syphillis, insanity, epilepsy and the "deficiency" of being an orphan.

While Galton slowly gained adherents for his ideas the science of criminal anthropology was being developed at the University of Turin by Cesare Lombroso, Professor of Legal Medicine. Lombroso believed that criminality was largely a matter of inheritance and could even be identified by physical characteristics. Thieves were small, had thick eyebrows, crooked noses and narrow foreheads. Sex criminals had bright eyes, high voices, blond hair and delicate faces. Murderers had glassy eyes, hooked noses, large cheeks, dark hair and long ears. While some people did not take Lombroso's "criminal characteristics" seriously the idea that one can inherit a predisposition to criminality was generally accepted throughout the scholarly world.

About the turn of the century, when the lecture circuit was the primary Saturday night entertainment in most American towns, the ideas of Galton and Lombroso were favorite lecture subjects in the United States. This interest is understandable in view of the great fear that the masses of "inferior" immigrants then coming to the United States would destroy the "purity" of American blood. To the Americans of British, German, Swedish or Irish descent the millions of Italians, Poles, Russians and east European Jews who came to this country at the turn of the century represented a threat to the "American way of life." These immigrants not only spoke a strange language and wore strange clothes, they seem to be addicted to crime, lived in horrible slums and bred huge families. Books such as *The Passing of a Great Race* by Madison Grant (a New York attorney, zoologist and leading advocate of compulsory programs of eugenic betterment) argued that the American people would soon die out because of the influx of inferior immigrants from eastern and southern Europe. Grant asserted that the White Anglo-Saxon Protestant (the true American) was:

> today being literally driven off the streets of New York by the swarms of Polish Jews. These immigrants adopt the language of the native American, they wear his clothes, they steal his name, they . . . take his women.[2]

This "threat" helped to produce the first attempts at eugenic legislation which provided for the sterilization of certain classes of defective persons. Generations of school children were told horror stories about such notorious families as the Jukes, the Nams, and the Kallikaks and were told that crime and poverty were matters of genetics.

In recent years the eugenic movement has lost much of its early racism. The discoveries of genetics, biological engineering, and sociology are acccepted and employed by eugenicists. Today, the thrust of the movement is toward advocacy of techniques which could raise the intellectual, artistic, moral and physical capacity of human beings. A consideration of the techniques of eugenics may help us to form some judgments on the legal and moral challenges posed by the efforts to improve the quality of life.

The Forcible Sterilization of the Defective

Compulsory eugenic sterilization is the one eugenic technique which has been widely employed in the United States. Thirty-one of the American states at one time had legislation which permitted the forced sterilization of designated classes of residents; twenty-five states currently retain this legislation. Courts have sometimes issued compulsory eugenic sterilization orders even without legislation. The intent of compulsory eugenic sterilization is obviously negative, i.e. to prevent defective children from being conceived by defective parents:

---

[2] Grant, *Passing of a Great Race*, p. 81. (1916).

It is the policy of the state to prevent the procreation and increase of feebleminded, insane and epileptic persons, idiots, imbeciles, moral degenerates, and sexual perverts likely to become a menace to society.[3]

Human nature will not be transformed or elevated to a higher level by compulsory eugenic sterilization, but would society be improved by its widespread application?

Since 1907 seventy-thousand Americans have been forcibly sterilized. Fifteen states still allow the sterilization of epileptics, two sterilize syphilitic persons, eight sterilize habitual criminals. Twenty-five states permit the sterilization of mental defectives, typically on the ground that the person is the "probable potential parent of socially inadequate offspring,"[4] or of "offspring with inherited inferior or anti-social traits."[5] But the use of compulsory eugenic sterilization has declined in recent years. There are a number of reasons for this decline. It is apparent that compulsory eugenic sterilization has not had any noticeable effect on the quality of society, even in states such as California and Indiana where it was widely used. The frightening abuse of compulsory eugenic sterilization by Nazi Germany showed how dangerous the technique could be in the hands of a racially prejudiced government. Indeed, in reversing an order for the sterilization of Otis Skinner, an "habitual criminal" chicken-stealer, Justice Douglas of the United States Supreme Court noted the dangers of compulsory eugenic sterilization:

We are dealing here with legislation which involves one of the basic civil rights of man. Marriage and procreation are fundamental to the very existence and survival of the race. The power to sterilize, if exercised, may have subtle, far-reaching and devastating effects. In evil or reckless hands it can cause races or types which are inimical to the dominant group to wither and disappear. There is no redemption for the individual whom the law touches. Any experiment which the State conducts is to his irreparable injury. He is forever de-

---

[3] Compiled Laws of Michigan ch. 720, section 301 (1948).
[4] West Virginia Code, ch. 16, section 1394.
[5] North Dakota Code, Title 23, section 0803.

prived of a basic liberty. We mention these matters not to
reexamine the scope of the police power of the States. We
advert to them merely in emphasis of our view that strict
scrutiny of the classification which a State makes in a sterilization law is essential, lest unwittingly, or otherwise, invidious
discriminations are made against groups or types of individuals
in violation of the constitutional guaranty of just and equal
laws.[6]

The early opposition to compulsory eugenic sterilization
was rarely based on theological grounds. Indeed, in the first
part of the twentieth century, some of the leading advocates
of compulsory eugenic sterilization were Christian clergymen.
Several American Catholic theologians wrote articles in support of the morality of the practice. But theological opposition
to compulsory eugenic sterilization began to grow as its im-
plausibility and dangers became apparent. In 1930 Pope Pius
XI denounced compulsory eugenic sterilization:

> Finally, that pernicious practice must be condemned which
> closely touches upon the natural right of man to enter matri-
> mony but affects also in a real way the welfare of the offspring.
> For there are some who, over-solicitous for the cause of
> eugenics, not only give salutary counsel for more certainly
> procuring the strength and health of the future child—which,
> indeed, is not contrary to right reason—but put eugenics before
> aims of a higher order, and by public authority wish to prevent
> from marrying all those who, even though naturally fit for
> marriage, they consider, according to the norms and conjec-
> tures of their investigations, would, through hereditary trans-
> mission, bring forth defective offspring. And more, they wish
> to legislate to deprive these of that natural faculty by medical
> action despite their unwillingness; and this they do not propose
> as an infliction of grave punishment under the authority of the
> State for a crime committed, nor to prevent future crimes by
> guilty persons, but against every right and good they wish the
> civil authority to arrogate to itself a power over faculty which
> it never had and can never legitimately possess.[7]

The Lambeth Conference of Anglican bishops condemned
the practice in 1958, and moralists have in recent years almost

---

[6] Skinner v. Oklahoma 316 U.S. 535 (1942).
[7] *Casti Connubii, Denz.* 3722, N.C.W.C. Translation.

unanimously denounced the technique. To allow the state to deny the fundamental human power of reproduction is to give the state absolute power over transmission of life. Aside from the humiliation, degradation, and shame suffered by the individual who is forced to surrender his reproductive powers, most moralists feel that compulsory eugenic sterilization is objectionable because of the power it places in the government.

The moralist's condemnation of a compulsory eugenic sterilization does not solve the problem of a judge who is confronted with a petition for sterilization. Can it be, that in this circumstance, sterilization would be the most humane, the most moral choice? In 1962 this question of law and conscience confronted a judge in Zanesville, Ohio. Nora Ann Simpson was an eighteen-year-old girl. She was pleasant and attractive, and was said to give the impression that she was normal. However, her I.Q. was only 36, and she had already given birth to one illegitimate child. Nora Ann's mother petitioned the judge to commit her to a mental hospital. Unfortunately, there were no vacancies in the institution. Mrs. Simpson then asked the judge to order Nora Ann sterilized for her own good, that of potential offspring and the good of society. The judge ordered Nora Ann sterilized even though no Ohio statute authorized him to do so. Before his decision is condemned, one must ask what alternatives were available to him. With the fate of Nora Ann in his hands could the judge have morally said "there is nothing I can do to help this feeble-minded girl?" But one can ask: "How does enforced sterilization help?

The Legal and Moral Implications of Artificial Insemination

In 1958 Lord Wheatley, a judge in Scotland, was confronted by a most unusual problem. A gentleman named MacLennan brought a suit for divorce against his wife on grounds of her adultery. MacLennan's evidence consisted of the fact that his wife had given birth to a baby girl notwithstanding the fact that the couple had not had sexual intercourse for over a year. Mrs. MacLennan contested the divorce suit. Her

defense admitted the truth of her husband's evidence but
argued that it did not prove adultery. Mrs. MacLennan alleged that she had introduced the semen of a donor into her
body with a syringe. Since she did not have intercourse with
the father of the child, Mrs. MacLennan argued that she had
not committed adultery. Lord Wheatley accepted Mrs. Mac-
Lennan's argument that artificial insemination of a married
woman, even without her husband's consent, was not adultery.
The judge's opinion reflects the concerns, confusion and problems which confront the law when it is faced with the application of scientific methods of life control to the traditional
values of family life:

> It is almost trite to say that a married woman who, without
> the consent of her husband, has the seed of a male donor
> injected into her person by mechanical means in order to
> procreate a child who would not be a child of the marriage has
> committed a grave and heinous breach of the contract of
> marriage. The question for my determination, however, is not
> the moral culpability of such an act but is whether such an
> act constitutes adultery in its legal meaning. A wife or a
> husband could commit an act of gross indecency with a mem-
> ber of the opposite sex which would be a complete violation
> of the marital relationship, but which could not be classified
> as adultery.
>
> In determining whether the marital offence (which I opine
> it to be whatever view one takes of its nature) of being im-
> pregnated by the seed of another man without the husband's
> consent constitutes adultery in its legal sense, one naturally
> seeks a solution from the definitions of "adultery" in the
> works of our leading legal writers or in reported decisions.
>
> Where, however, attempts were made to describe adultery
> if not to provide an exhaustive definition of it, the idea of
> conjunctio corporum seems to be an inherent concomitant—
> a conception of the process which incidentally can likewise be
> found in the book of Deuteronomy, the writings of St. Paul
> and the works of the Canonists. The idea that adultery might
> be committed by a woman alone in the privacy of her bedroom
> aided and abetted only by a syringe containing semen was one
> with which the earlier jurists had no occasion to wrestle.
> Certainly this form of perpetuation of the species does not
> conform to the common conception of adultery. Nonetheless

the argument advanced in support of the contention that it does constitute adultery was powerfully advanced.

In the normal and natural method of performing an act of sexual intercourse there is a mutual surrender both of the sexual and reproductive organs. While the primary purpose of sexual intercourse is procreation, in the eyes of the law surrender of the reproductive organs is not necessary to consummate the act of intercourse. Expedients may be used by the parties to secure birth prevention or the woman may have previously undergone an operation by which her reproductive organs were removed, or they may have ceased to function from natural causes and yet the conjunction of the sexual organs involving at least some degree of penetration would constitute intercourse and, in the circumstances under consideration, adultery. Thus impregnation per se cannot be a test of adultery, since in the eyes of the law the act of intercourse can be consummated without impregnation either as a result of natural causes or by the parties resorting to artificial expedients . . . It would seem, therefore that in determining such questions as consummation of marriage or adultery, the law looks at the act and not the result.

Although not presented in syllogistic form the pursuer's argument seemed to be that in the given circumstances while undoubtedly all cases of penetration of the female organ by the male organ were adultery even if impregnation did not take place, so too all cases of impregnation were adultery even if there was no such penetration. This to my mind is a legal non sequitur. The argument seems to me to confuse the method with the result. Impregnation may be the result of sexual intercourse, but is not necessarily an essential part of it, and if it is achieved by other means which do not involve the physical presence of the male and his sexual organ, it is difficult to see how such other means can be classified as sexual intercourse or to use the more significant phrase "carnal connection."

If the view be taken, as I think it must, that gross indecency short of sexual intercourse is not adultery, however reprehensible it may be, then there must be some defining line between the two, and it is for that reason that Courts in England seem to have insisted that some degree of penetration must have occurred before sexual intercourse can be said to have taken place.

. . . I . . . derive . . . the following propositions, according at least to the law of England.

1. For adultery to be committed there must be the two

parties physically present and engaging in the sexual act at the same time.

2. To constitute the sexual act there must be an act of union involving some degree of penetration of the female organ by the male organ.

3. It is not a necessary concomitant of adultery that male seed should be deposited in the female's ovum.

4. The placing of the male seed in the female ovum need not necessarily result from the sexual act, and if it does not, but is placed there by some other means, there is no sexual intercourse.

* * *

. . . Just as artificial insemination extracts procreation entirely from the nexus of human relationships in or outside of marriage, so does the extraction of the nexus of human relationship from the act of procreation remove artificial insemination from the classification of sexual intercourse. If my views be correct, then it follows logically that artificial insemination by a donor without the consent of the husband is not adultery as the law interprets that term.

The idea that a woman is committing adultery when alone in the privacy of her bedroom she injects into her ovum by means of a syringe the seed of a man whom she does not know and has never seen is one which I am afraid I cannot accept. Unilateral adultery is possible, as in the case of a married man who ravishes a woman not his wife, but self-adultery is a conception as yet unknown to the law. The argument of pursuer's counsel was that adultery meant the introduction of a foreign element into the marital relationship. That, however, seems to me to beg the question, because what has still to be determined is what is the foreign element? For the reasons which I have already explained, that foreign element is the physical contact with an alien and unlawful sexual organ, and without that element there cannot be what the law regards as adultery. The introduction of a spurious element into the family, with all its consequences, may be the result of such conduct, but is not a necessary result, and it is by the means and not by the result that this issue is to be judged.[8]

The technique used by Mrs. MacLennan to make herself pregnant has long been known. That it has eugenic possibili-

---

[8] MacLennan v. MacLennan [1958] Scots Law Times 12.

ties is apparent from the fact that artificial insemination has been used for decades to breed superior livestock. Professor Herman Muller has suggested that voluntary germinal choice through artificial insemination by donor (A.I.D.) is the best method of eugenic advancement presently available.

Artificial insemination by donor has been used to conceive several hundred thousand Americans, but only rarely has its use been eugenically motivated. If Muller's proposal is to be effective, radical changes would have to be made in the practice of artificial insemination by donor. Artificial insemination is most commonly used today when the husband is sterile. The physician secures the donor's sperm, frequently in a haphazard way. Strict secrecy dominates the procedure; few, if any, records are preserved. The average physician has little understanding of genetic theory. Usually, the physician is more concerned with producing a child which "looks like" the husband than in a genetically superior child. The well known leader of the Planned Parenthood group, Dr. Alan Guttmacher, has proposed a set of rules for the administration of artificial insemination by donor which is not contributive to eugenic progress in the opinion of many geneticists:

(1) the donor must be anonymous;
(2) the physician must personally know the couple seeking artificial insemination by donor;
(3) the physician should discourage the use of the technique;
(4) no paper, contracts or records should be kept;
(5) the physician administering artificial insemination by donor should also deliver the child;
(6) medical fees of the techniques should be low.[9]

It should be obvious that Guttmacher is here speaking for the physician who desires to use the technique according to the wishes of his patient, but is not particularly interested in the eugenic implications of the practice. Donor anonymity and the absence of records would prevent any compilation of

---

[9] Summarized from Guttmacher, "Artificial Insemination," 97 Ann. New York Acad. Sciences 623 (1962).

statistical data necessary to meaningful eugenic use of artificial insemination by donor. Guttmacher also seems uninterested in the legal problem of the potential illegitimacy of an artificial insemination by donor child. Thus he would destroy all evidence that the husband is not the biological father.

Those who advocate eugenic use of artificial insemination by donor argue that medical use of the technique must undergo radical reform. The technique could be used to avoid transmitting the husband's genetic defects to the child or to overcome some constitutional trait in the husband which is incompatible with a trait in the wife. If neither of these problems exist, the eugenicists would still urge a couple to make a choice by using the sperm of a donor who is intellectually, physically, or artistically superior to the husband. If artificial insemination by donor is to have eugenic uses, donors must be chosen with care, and their sperm must be classified according to their genetic strengths and weaknesses. Detailed records of the subsequent histories of all parties involved should be kept. The collection of the data would eventually begin to reveal the strengths and weaknesses of artificial insemination by donor. Since it is now possible to freeze and store spermatozoa almost indefinitely, there is no reason why eugenically orientated sperm-banks could not become realities. Professor Muller has said that germinal choice by eugenic artificial insemination by donor is a highly moral act of great social responsibility. Few people believe that today. Unless a substantial part of society comes to believe it in the future there is little chance that voluntary artificial insemination by donor would become a tool of eugenic progress.

Compulsory Artificial Insemination and Governmental Policy

Over a decade ago L. Kubie asked in the *Saturday Review*: "Who is going to license young folk to exercise the precious right to procreate?" The question may remain a preposterous one for several generations. But many serious scientific writers have struggled with the thought that on some not-too-distant day in the future, governments may attempt to control the reproductive process through techniques such as compulsory artificial insemination by donor. The problem of compulsion will be examined below in relation to law and morals. But it is apparent that a state which developed a sufficiently large bank of sperm from superior donors could attempt to draw a eugenic blueprint of the next generation. The practical and legal problems inherent in any attempt to limit reproduction to the artificial insemination by donor techniques would be staggering. However, it is also impossible to appreciate the communications and educational techniques which governments may someday control in order to coerce the minds and judgments of their citizens. The very failure of theologians, philosophers, lawyers and sociologists to consider the implications of current practices of artificial insemination by donor could probably contribute to the atmosphere in which a government could propagate a program of eugenic transformation through compulsory germinal selection.

Among the most serious of legal and moral problems created by artificial insemination by donor are those relating to the structure of the family. Is the technique legally or morally desirable from the viewpoint of the husband-wife relationship? What is the relationship of the husband to the child? Is artificial insemination by donor compatible with the Judeo-Christian understanding of family life or to the monogamous marriage theory which permeates the whole legal structure of the American family? In examining these questions one is brought face to face with the problem of the fundamental legal and moral structure of family life. If for no other reason, artificial insemination by donor should be a catalyst for the re-evaluation of the family by both legal scholars and moralists.

Artificial Insemination and the Judeo-Christian View of Marriage

For the Christian Jesus has defined marital love as a life of total self-giving unity: "So they are no longer two but one"

(Mt 19:5). This definition, in turn, reflects the Jewish view of marriage. Said man to woman in the ancient text of Genesis:

> "This at last is the bone of my bones and flesh of my flesh" (Gen 2:23).

When a woman has herself impregnated with the sperm of a man who is not her husband has she breached the sacred trust of marital love? If the husband approves of the artificial insemination by donor, has he defiled his marriage? To some, the answer to these questions is an emphatic no. They maintain that the mere introduction of the donor as the biological father in no way diminishes the unity of husband and wife. To hold otherwise would be to place too much emphasis on the merely physical dimensions of the husband-wife relationship, according to this view. The problem with this answer is that the husband-wife relationship is the sign and reality of loving communion. To say that artificial insemination by donor is a "mere physical intrusion" into the marriage is not to remove but to create moral objections. While artificial insemination by donor would not constitute adultery according to the traditional definitions of moral theology it has the same effect on the family structure as adultery. When the sperm of a donor is used to remedy some inadequacy of the husband, a third party has entered the man-woman relationship at one of its most fundamental points: the giving of existence to children. The basic moral error of adultery is that one of the parties to a marriage seeks some satisfaction in a third party which the spouse cannot provide. Artificial insemination by donor is not adultery only in the technical sense that it involves no intercourse. It is adulterous in the sense that it permits the introduction of a third party into the marital relation at a fundamental point in order to remedy an inadequacy of one of the spouses. Such conduct is unjustifiable from the viewpoint of the Judeo-Christian understanding of the interpersonal character of marital life.

Perhaps the most cogent statement of the incompatibility of Judeo-Christian marriage with artificial insemination by donor was made by Pope XII in an address of October 29, 1951:

> To reduce the cohabitation of married persons and the conjugal act to a mere organic function for the transmission of the germ of life would be to convert the domestic hearth, sanctuary of the family, into nothing more than a biological laboratory. Hence, in our address of September 29, 1949, to the international congress of Catholic doctors, we formally excluded artificial insemination from marriage. The conjugal act in its natural structure is a personal action, a simultaneous and immediate co-operation of the spouses, which by the very nature of the participants and the special character of the act, is the expression of that mutual self-giving which, in the words of Holy Scripture, effects the union in one flesh.[10]

Artificial Insemination and the Legal Structures of Marital Life

In the MacLennan case Lord Wheatley decided that artificial insemination by donor did not constitute adultery. From a historical point of view actual intercourse between a spouse and a third party is needed for adultery. "Even actual proof of sex conduct (short of adultery) with a third party is not tantamount to adultery."[11]

Definition of adultery in terms of intercourse has sometimes been criticized by legal commentators, but until the advent of artificial insemination by donor the definition stood. Artificial insemination by donor now raises serious problems with the definition. One of the reasons for adultery prohibitions, both as a punishable crime and as grounds for divorce, is the

---

[10] A.A.S. 835 (Oct. 29, 1951).
[11] W. v. W., 226 A. 2d 860 (1967).

possibility that the adulterous wife could introduce into her spouse's legal bloodline a child who in fact was conceived by another man. Legal approval of artificial insemination by donor would have the effect of permitting this. Even if a requirement that the husband's consent were introduced into such legislation, a rather basic legal aspect of the husband-wife-child relationship would collapse. The desirability and/or effect of such a collapse has yet to be seriously debated by legal scholars.

Another reason for the prohibition of adultery in the law is the belief that the unity of husband and wife should create an exclusive physical relationship between them. In this, the law no doubt reflects western society's deep-seated conviction that marriage requires a man and a woman to be totally and exclusively one with each other for the good which the commonweal receives from the union.

Is artificial insemination by donor such an intrusion into the exclusivity of sexual-reproductive powers which husband and wife share as to constitute an adulterous intrusion? The English House of Lords was faced with this problem in the 1924 case of *Russell v. Russell*. Mr. Russell had been granted a divorce when he testified that in spite of his wife's pregnancy he never had intercourse with her. The trial judge found that Mrs. Russell had been made pregnant by the sperm of another man with whom she had not had actual intercourse. The court quaintly referred to this as a "fecundation *ab extra*." The House of Lords reversed this finding because it was based on incompetent evidence, but Lord Dunedin's analysis was that "fecundation *ab extra* is, I doubt not, adultery."

Dunedin's dictum can be supported, for the introduction of the third party's sperm into the body of the wife is an actual physical intrusion in the marriage which cannot be justified in the context of monogamous marriage. However, there are few cases in which the question has been considered.

In 1945 a Mr. Hoch sued his wife for divorce in Chicago,

Illinois. Mrs. Hoch had become pregnant while her husband was in the military service. Mrs. Hoch's defense to the charge of adultery was based on her testimony that she had become pregnant through artificial insemination by donor. Judge Feinberg granted the divorce on other evidence of Mrs. Hoch's adultery, but gave an opinion that artificial insemination by donor was not adultery even though the husband did not consent.

The first case to present a court with the problem of artificial insemination by donor occurred in Canada in 1921.[12] A Mrs. Orford sued her husband for support. Mr. Orford resisted the claim on the grounds that his wife had committed adultery. The marriage had never been consumated because of the wife's alleged inability to have sexual intercourse. A physician had advised the wife that the birth of a child would help to cure her impotency. The wife alleged that she separated from her husband, went to England, and was there subjected to the technique of artificial insemination by donor. At the time the child was born Mrs. Orford had not seen her husband for more than three years. The court rejected Mrs. Orford's story, finding that she had committed adultery "in the ordinary, natural way." However, in an interesting dictum, the court discussed the defense of artificial insemination by donor. The judge wrote that artificial insemination by donor is adultery. "The essence of the offense of adultery consists, not in the moral turpitude of the act of sexual intercourse, but in the voluntary surrender to another person of the reproductive powers or faculties of the guilty person; and any submission of those powers to the service or enjoyment of any other person than the husband or wife comes within the definition of adultery."

The Orford case focuses on a vital legal problem created by artificial insemination by donor: is the technique objectionable because it introduces a third party between the husband and wife in the sexual-reproductive function of the family?

---

[12] Orford v. Orford, 49 Ont. L.R. 15, (1921).

Artificial Insemination and the Legal Structure of the Parent-Child Relationship

A child conceived through artificial insemination by donor will not know his biological father; he will know the husband of his mother as his father. One might be superficially tempted to compare him to an adopted son. In 1948 a divorce case presented a New York judge with the opportunity to analyze the relationship between the husband and the child conceived by the wife through artificial insemination. A Mr. Strnad asked the judge to grant him the right to visit the child which had been conceived by Mrs. Strnad with the sperm of a donor. Strnad had consented to the technique. The judge granted the request for visitation rights, accepting the proposition that the consent to artificial insemination by donor constituted a "semi-adoption." The judge also said that the child was the legitimate offspring of Mr. and Mrs. Strnad even though conceived with a donor's sperm.

In 1963 another New York judge ruled that a child conceived through artificial insemination by donor was illegitimate. Mrs. Gursky sought an annulment from Mr. Gursky on the grounds that he was impotent and unable to consummate the marriage. The couple had one child by means of artificial insemination by donor. The court held that the child was illegitimate in spite of Gursky's consent to the procedure, but ordered him to support the child anyway. An Illinois judge had previously ruled that a child conceived by artificial insemination was illegitimate. Mrs. Doornbos sought a court order awarding her sole custody of the child. She argued that since Mr. Doornbos was not the biological father of the child he had no legal interest in it. The judge agreed with Mrs. Doornbos, stating that artificial insemination by donor is contrary to public policy of the family law of Illinois.

In a New York family law proceeding in 1958, a judge refused to let a wife testify that her children had been conceived through artificial insemination by donor. The couple had received a Nevada divorce decree. The wife argued that the husband had no interest in the children because they had been conceived with the sperm of an unknown donor. The court ordered her to permit visitation and prevented the wife from even proving her charges of an artificial insemination by donor:

> To stigmatize them as children of an unknown father by means of artificial insemination of the mother is no more, in my view, than at attempt to make these innocents out as children of bastardy. And where a parent attempts such means the law will still the lips of such a parent.[13]

But in 1967, in a California court, a husband was permitted to show that a child born to his wife was not his but was conceived through artificial insemination by donor. Folmer Sorensen was being prosecuted for non-support of the child; the court ruled that he could not be prevented from showing the insemination. Sorensen had consented to the insemination, but if he was not permitted to show that the child had a different father he would be punished for failing to support another man's child.

That spouses will sometimes use artificial insemination for reasons other than a desire for a child further confuses the parent-child relationship. In 1949, an English judge had such a case before him. A woman asked for an annulment because of her husband's psychic impotency. During five years of married life the husband had been unable to have intercourse with the wife. A physician suggested that if the couple would have a child the husband might learn to relax and have sexual coitus. The physician used the husband's sperm (not a donor's) to artificially impregnate the wife. A child was conceived, but the husband's impotency persisted. When the husband then attempted to use the crude techniques for consummation suggested by a psychologist, the wife sought the annulment. The husband resisted the suit on the theory that the annulment would illegitimize the child even though it was admittedly the product of his genetic material. The judge granted the annulment, explaining that "the future holds

---

13 Abajian v. Dennett 184 N.Y.S. 2d 178 (1958).

better for the child . . . if I grant the decree than if he is brought up by an embittered mother who may for life be tied to a marriage that has never been a real marriage and which, only through the unnatural aid of science, has produced the fruit of a real marriage."[14]

To many people the law of illegitimacy is an absurdity. To one without legal training calling a child "illegitimate" is cruelty. This attitude is actually a commentary not on law but on a misunderstanding of the law. Legitimacy is a legal fiction, not a moral judgment. The fiction has well-defined historical purpose in the law of inheritance and child support. The primary purpose of the fiction is to structure the legal relationship of a child to its parents. Even judges sometimes fail to appreciate that illegitimacy is not a social or moral stigma on a child. More than 10% of the children born in the United States today are illegitimate. It is important to appreciate this, and for society to cease using the illegitimacy fiction as a stigma. However, illegitimacy is and must remain a viable concept for a society which accepts specified patterns of family life as desirable. Unless American society is prepared to separate biological paternity from family life it must see artificial insemination by donor as creating illegitimacy.

The Implications of Sperm and Ovum Banks

The legal and moral problems raised by artificial insemination by donor to some extent carry over into similar techniques for reproduction. It is possible to take an ovum from a female donor and transplant it to the body of the wife where it would be available for impregnation by the husband's sperm. Ovum banks and sperm banks may, in the future, provide a couple with the complete genetic material needed to place a child in the womb of the mother. In fact, when the need for pregnancy is eliminated by an artificial womb outside the woman, a couple will be able to choose the genetic ma-

---

[14] R.E.L. v. E.L. [1949] p. 211.

terial of the child, have it deposited in the hospital for development, and pick up a viable child a few months later.

Professor Teh Ping Lin of the University of California has shown that outside material can be successfully injected into fertilized mouse ova which can then be implanted into a female mouse other than the original mother. This opens the possibility of altering the genetic composition of a stored egg before it is implanted into a woman or artificial womb. Dr. Robert Edwards of Baltimore has already proven that human ova can mature outside the body of a woman to the point where they are available for fertilization.

The effect that these developments may have on the structures of current family life is incalculable. The greatest problem raised by these developments centers around the power to create life outside of familial institutions. By careful selection, classification and manipulation of genetic materials, the state could produce an entire generation of specified types. That this could be accomplished outside the family, completely under the direction of state agencies, staggers the mind of anyone who believes that the family is the center of man's social existence. The moral and legal ramifications of this problem have been ignored by all except a few thoughtful biologists. Those who are interested in family life from the view-point of legal-social-moral structures had better begin to consider such developments seriously.

The Bishops of the Second Vatican Council proclaimed that "Parents should regard as their proper mission the task of transmitting human life and educating those to whom it has been transmitted." Developments in molecular biology may make that statement obsolete unless man can be totally convinced that the family is the only proper vehicle for the transmission of life.

Asexual Reproduction

In *The Authentic Morality* Father Ignace Lepp's analysis of male masturbation indicates that some modern sexual taboos grew out of man's overestimation of the importance

of the male seed in reproduction. Far from being the sole
agent of reproduction, as ancient man believed, the sperm
may not even be a necessary agent. Research has indicated
that clonal reproduction may be possible among human beings; that is, biologists may someday be able to grow people
or organs from a small cluster of cells. In fact, female ova
have reproduced through manipulation of the genetic material. Many biologists believe that human females have conceived and given birth to children without the insemination
by a male sperm. Parthenogenesis is a distinct possibility
because the sperm is only a stimulus. The female has within
the ova the full means of reproduction if some substitute for
the male stimulus can be found. If techniques for induced
parthenogenesis became available, the functional value of the
human male would diminish. It is possible that a government might attempt to build a eugenic blueprint based on
parthenogenesis. However, distinguished biologists such as
Theodosius Dobzhansky have indicated that sexual reproduction became established among humans because it provided
the best technique for adaptation and progressive evolution.
A leading Christian philosopher, Jean Guitton, has suggested
that sexual reproduction may have some clear eugenic advan-
tages over parthenogenesis:

> It is evident that sexuality favours the variability of the
> species. If the parent belonged to only one type of being, the
> product would be identical with that which begot it; daughters
> who were daughters of their mother alone would resemble her
> in every respect. Moreover, all the variations which could be
> produced in the maternal chromosomes would reappear in the
> second generation and so on indefinitely. It is probable that,
> under these conditions, the species would disappear through
> impoverishment and perhaps also through degradation; for,
> in hereditary transmission, the bad generally prevails over the
> good. The aberrant and monstrous forms which appear so
> frequently in the existing world would occur more frequently
> still and that without any mechanism which could neutralise
> them.
>
> Suppose, on the contrary, that an individual derive from
> two parents, the one male, the other female, that he possess

two different heredities and that this be repeated in each generation: the potentialities which are in the species and, in some manner, materialised in the chromosomes, will then group themselves in every possible combination and at the same time be capable of mutual compensation. The two fundamental needs of life, the permanence of the type and the variability of individuals, will thus be better assured; above all new, original and creative combinations, like the highest prizes in a lottery, have the chance of being drawn.

Sex-differentiation thus corresponds to that of the two functions necessary for development: the female represents heredity and identity: she is the race, permanence; the male, on the other hand, guarantees the variations. And the combination of the two factors makes progress possible, above all if the permanence is sufficiently strong to prevent the variations from changing the type. It will be said that monstrosity is eliminated by life, whereas genius is favoured by the better adaptation which it enjoys.[15]

Man and the Direction of Evolution

Developments in biology indicate that in the near future man will have in his possession power to alter the very nature of life. This power staggers the imagination of contemporary man and dictates the need to develop legal and moral categories to deal with it. The Nobel-laureate geneticist Joshua Lederberg has proposed three possible routes by which man could transform life. First, man could alter the individual genes of the fertilized ovum. This could be done to destroy genetic defects or to produce some desirable characteristics. The second route is probably much closer to technical realization than the first. This involves an alteration of the genetic composition of an existing individual and has sometimes been called "genetic surgery" (Lederberg calls it "euphenics"). This modification might be accomplished through chemical agents. Such surgery could not only eliminate hereditary defects in an existing person, but could transform him into a physically or mentally superior being.

---

[15] Guitton, *Human Love*, Chicago; Franciscan Herald Press, (1966).

A third method by which nature might be transformed through human agency is body-cell genetics. Each cell of the human body contains the means by which the development of life is directed, D.N.A. If the D.N.A. from a cell of the body were taken and placed into an ovum, an exact duplicate of the person from whose body the cell was taken would develop. If the technical means for sustaining this life while it is developing were available, either duplicate organs (useful for transplant operations as old organs need replacement) or an entire duplicate human being could be produced. Dr. James of the California Institute of Technology has said that duplicates of human beings could be produced in a laboratory as early as 1983 if an intensive program based on present knowledge were undertaken. The work of Dr. Arthur Kornberg, the Nobel Prize biochemist who made a living virus in the laboratory, just begins to indicate the future potential in this area of research. It is foreseeable that scientists will someday produce beings with the best features of human and lower animal life by the crossing of cells from human bodies and other animals. The various forms of intelligent life which could result outstrip the wildest imaginings of contemporary man. It is for good reason that Olaf Stapledon has foreseen a day in the twenty-first century when not only will man have achieved super-intelligence but lower forms of animal life will have achieved the level of intelligence and artistry now enjoyed by man.

Biologists uniformly agree that in the future these or similar techniques will enable man to transform not only the world around him but himself as well. Mutation of man's genetic composition will enable him to transform his nature into forms of his own choosing. This raises the most fearsome moral challenge of transformationist eugenics: how should man make himself over? The form of human nature is not predestined; if man chooses to make himself over *what* should he make of himself? Just as the engineering sciences have drastically affected the physical structures man uses for his daily needs and conveniences, the application of engineering principles to advances in bio-chemistry will no doubt create the ability to effect mass transformation of man. A Soviet scientist recently described the growing interest in the partnership between bio-chemistry and engineering:

> The results of biological research have come to be of interest to sciences like cybernetics or bionics, having direct egresses into engineering . . . This opens great prospects for the acceleration and intensification of the general process by which science is converted into a direct productive force of society.

What is the quality of human life which man should produce? What are the social, intellectual, artistic, physical and spiritual qualities man should attempt to develop in himself through techniques of bio-chemical engineering?

Many men refuse even to consider such questions. Some feel the questions are absurd. The believer may feel that even to ask such questions is to assume the place of God. Disturbing as the question may be, the believer cannot ignore them when man will shortly possess the power which will make these considerations immediate moral challenges rather than science-fiction speculations. If the believer does not begin to contribute to the life-control debate now, he will leave the eugenic movement to those whose philosophy may not reflect the Judeo-Christian reverence for life. The believer can impress on the eugenic movement his belief in the inherent God-like dignity of each man, regardless of that man's physical, intellectual or spiritual deficiency, only if now he begins to contribute to the dialogue over man's eugenic transformation. He can contribute nothing if he hides from the question science is asking.

The challenge of Genesis is the Creator's placing of man in a place of dominance over nature:

> God said, "Let us make man in our image, in the likeness of ourselves, and let them be masters of the fish of the sea, the birds of heaven, the cattle, all the wild beasts, and all the reptiles that crawl upon the earth." God created man in the image of himself, in the image of God he created him, male and female he created them. God blessed them, saying to

them, "Be fruitful, multiply, fill the earth and conquer it"
(Gen 1:26–28).

Is the bold effort to take hold of nature and transform it
inherently contrary to the Judeo-Christian ethic? It is not. In
fact, transformationist eugenics gives man his greatest opportunity to share in the Genesis challenge of creation. It is
only when compulsion is used or the particular technique
contradicts some basic moral value that transformationist
eugenics becomes objectionable.

Compulsory Transformationist Eugenic Policies

If there is any one possibility in the future of transformationist eugenics which should frighten and disturb, it is the
proposal that techniques of improvement should be imposed
by force on the population. The advocates of compulsory
eugenic techniques propose to make the genetic development
of mankind less haphazard than it would be if mankind continued reproducing on the basis of purely monogamous marriage. True progress, they believe, can come about only when
man blueprints his genetic future and then introduces social
controls which will compel a following of the blueprint. The
blueprint must be so comprehensive that both the elimination
of genetic defects and the increase of superior genetic endow-
ments will result.

The compulsory techniques which might be employed can
only be guessed at. Dr. John R. Platt of the University of
Michigan Health Research Institute has suggested that in the
future human reproduction might be controlled by mass-
produced contraceptive agents placed in foodstuffs. Bio-
chemical agents which produce certain eugenic results might
similarly be given to the entire population through governmental control of food distribution. Newly conceived children, or even adults who are potential parents, might be forced
to undergo some form of genetic surgery aimed at transform-
ing their genetic constitutions. The potential governmental
techniques for forced eugenic transformation far exceed com-

pulsory eugenic sterilization, required artificial insemination by donor, or compulsory eugenic abortion. One can envision governmental agencies whose sole function is to direct the production of certain forms of human life. If this excites fear in the human heart, it is with good reason. P. B. Medawar has suggested that consciously employed socially-organized techniques of eugenic improvement can be carried out only in a dictatorship such as Nazi Germany. Compulsory eugenic techniques are inherently regressive because they necessarily involve political considerations as to who is a desirable person and who is not. In such an atmosphere fundamental human freedoms, proclaimed both by the Judeo-Christian tradition and the Anglo-American legal system, would quickly wither away.

In the end analysis, however sympathic one may be to the goals of transformationist eugenics, the believer and the man of law will resist any proposal that would give to the state the power to compel participation. Perhaps the Bishops of the Second Vatican Council have best expressed the reason that compulsion is an unsatisfactory means of improving human life:

> A sense of the dignity of the human person has been impressing itself more and more deeply on the consciousness of contemporary man. And the demand is increasingly made that men should act on their own judgment, enjoying and making use of a responsible freedom, not driven by coercion but motivated by a sense of duty. The demand is also made that constitutional limits should be set to the powers of government, in order that there may be no encroachment on the rightful freedom of the person and of associations. This demand for freedom in human society chiefly regards the quest for the values proper to the human spirit (*Declaration on Religious Freedom* §1).

In *The Biological Time Bomb*,[16] Gordon Taylor recently asked searching and thoughtful questions about the direction in which the biologist is taking the race. He also indicated

---

[16] Cleveland: World Publishing Co., 1968.

clearly that moral systems which oppose change on the basis of "pre-rational tribal taboos" will become irrelevant in their ability to influence the future of man. This is why it is important for advocates of the Judeo-Christian ethic to examine the developments in the light of fundamental beliefs and not simply to oppose change and experiment on the basis of ancient prejudices.

It may be true, as Teilhard de Chardin has observed in the *Phenomenon of Man*, that "modern man no longer knows what to do with the powers he has unleashed, the control of which he now holds in his hands." But if man begins now to ponder seriously the bio-chemical power he holds over his own reproductive capacity, he may be able to fulfill the observation of the psalmist:

> You have made him little less than a god, you have crowned him with glory and splendor, made him lord over the work of your hands, set all things under his feet (Psalm 8:5–6).

CHAPTER II

THE DILEMMA OF EUGENIC ABORTION

Can Life Be Improved By Destroying The Defective?

In the mid-sixties a young boy filed a most extraordinary personal injury suit in the court of New Jersey. Jeffrey Gleitman had been born with serious defects of sight, hearing and speech. He sued the physician who had cared for his mother during pregnancy. The defendant, Dr. Cosgrove, knew that Mrs. Gleitman had been infected with German measles in the early stages of pregnancy. Jeffrey's complaint alleged that Cosgrove's failure to warn Mrs. Gleitman that the infection might harm her unborn child caused her to carry Jeffrey to full term. Jeffrey argued that Cosgrove's alleged negligence prevented him from being aborted and thus forced him to live a life burdened with terrible physical deficiencies. The suit was dismissed. In March, 1967, the Supreme Court of New Jersey answered the dilemma posed by Jeffrey's suit:

> the infant plaintiff would have us measure the difference between his life with defects against the utter void of non-existence. This court cannot weigh the value of life with impairments against the non-existence of life itself. . . . It is basic to the human condition to seek life and hold on to it however heavily burdened. If Jeffrey could have been asked as to whether his life should be snuffed out before his full term of gestation could run its course, our felt intuition of human nature tells us he almost surely would choose life with defects as against no life at all. "For the living there is hope, but for the dead there is none." Theocritus . . . *The right to life is inalienable in our society . . . Eugenic considerations are not*

controlling. We are not talking here about the breeding of prize cattle.[1]

Underlying Jeffrey Gleitman's argument is the proposition that death is better than life with serious defects. The response of the Supreme Court of New Jersey to this proposition reflects a traditional western appreciation of the value of human life. But even in the western world there have been men who believed that the best cure for social or physical defects is to kill the defective. Euthanasia of the old or infirm, with or without their consent, is not unknown even in twentieth century America. In October, 1968, a jury in Brooklyn, New York, awarded a judgment of $110,000 to Mr. and Mrs. Robert Stewart who had been refused an abortion by the defendant New York hospital; the unaborted child, Rosalyn, was born blind, deaf, spastic, and mentally retarded. Medieval theologians taught that non-repentant heretics should be killed by the state to prevent them from destroying the teaching of the Church. Popes granted indulgences to those who went on Crusades to kill "infidel" Moselms. Today there are Christians who propose that the solution to communism is to kill communists. Notwithstanding these aberrations, the Judeo-Christian ethic has long been considered incompatible with the proposition that the unfit are unworthy of life. "You must not put the innocent and the just to death" (Dan 13:53) has remained the strongest argument for not taking the life of a human being simply because he is socially, physically or mentally defective.

In the twentieth century there are some who argue that both Christian and western ethics have become so community-orientated that the right of a defective person to live should be subordinated to the needs and/or conveniences of society. Undoubtedly, hard cases cause the community-orientated person to wonder whether this might not be true. For example, the seriously defective child whose needs drain the material, emotional and spiritual energies of the family

---

[1] Gleitman v. Cosgrove 227 A.2d 689 (1961).

community: is there a point at which the survival of the family requires the destruction of the child?

Illustrating this problem is the case of a man named Repouille. Repouille filed a petition for naturalization as an American citizen in 1944; federal law requires that such a petitioner be of "good moral character" in the five years preceding the filing. Repouille, within the five years, had been convicted of manslaughter. When a federal district court ordered Repouille naturalized, the Immigration and Naturalization service appealed. The opinion of the federal appeals court revoking the order of naturalization cogently states the tragic circumstances of Repouille's conduct and examines the moral-legal implications of eugenic euthanasia. Judge Hand wrote the opinion:

> On October 12, 1939, he (Repouille) had deliberately put to death his son, a boy of thirteen by means of chloroform. His reason for this tragic deed was that the child had suffered from birth from a brain injury which destined him to be an idiot and a physical monstrosity malformed in all four limbs. The child was blind, mute, and deformed. He had to be fed; the movements of his bladder and bowels were involuntary, and his entire life was spent in a small crib. Repouille had four other children at the time towards whom he has always been dutiful and responsible; it may be assumed that his act was to help him in their nurture, which was being compromised by the burden imposed upon him in the care of the fifth. The family was altogether dependent upon his industry for its support. He was indicted for a manslaughter in the first degree; but the jury brought in a verdict of manslaughter in the second degree with a recommendation of the utmost clemency; the defendant was placed on probation.
>
> There are great numbers of people of the most unimpeachable virtue, who think it morally justifiable to put an end to life so inexorably destined to be a burden to others, —and—so far as any possible interest of its own is concerned—condemned to a brutish existence, lower indeed than all but the lowest forms of sentient life. Nor is it inevitably an answer to say that it must be immoral to do this, until the law provides security against the abuses which would inevitably follow, unless the practice were regulated. Many people—probably most people—do not make it a final ethical act

of ourselves or of others the unflinching obedience of a Socrates. There being no lawful means of accomplishing an end, which they believe to be righteous in itself, there have always been conscientious persons who feel no scruple in their personal convictions, and who even regard as martyrs those who suffer by doing so. In our own history it is only necessary to recall the Abolitionists. It is reasonably clear that the jury which tried Repouille did not feel any moral repulsion at his crime.

One might be tempted to seize upon all this as a reliable measure of current morals; but we should hesitate to accept it as decisive, when, for example, we compare it with the fate of a similar offender in Massachusetts, who, although he was not executed, was imprisoned for life.

We can say no more than that, quite independently of what may be the current moral feeling as to legally administered euthanasia, we feel reasonably secure in holding that only a minority of virtuous persons would deem the practice morally justifiable, while it remains in private hands, even when the provocation is as overwhelming as it was in this instance.[2]

Infanticide has been practiced in many civilizations. It has been said to exist in some modern American hospitals where a child born with serious physical deformities is sometimes left unattended by the staff in order to insure his rapid death. Every so often a dramatic case of infanticide will focus attention on the moral and legal implications of the practice. Such a case arose in Belgium in the early sixties when a mother killed her defective child a few days after birth. The general public cheered the jury's verdict of acquittal, but in the following months serious doubts about the ultimate wisdom of the verdict were voiced. A mother kills her child because she loves the baby—or is there another motive buried deep in the unconscious? Whatever the motive, lofty or base, can the law approve the taking of one person's life by another?

Of the diverse forms of euthanasia known to human history the most widely discussed today is eugenic abortion. A famous case in which this technique was employed occurred in the early sixties. Mrs. Sherri Finkbine of Arizona had taken

---

2 Repouille v. United States 165 F.2d 152 (1947).

a drug containing thalidomide in the early stages of pregnancy. Shortly after she took this drug the Federal government barred thalidomide from import or distribution in the United States on the grounds that the compound caused fetal deformities. Mrs. Finkbine's request for an abortion was rejected by physicians on the grounds that such an operation would be illegal in Arizona. Mrs. Finkbine then filed a suit asking for court declaration on the status of eugenic abortion under Arizona law; the suit was dismissed. Mrs. Finkbine then went to Sweden where the abortion was performed. The debate among moralists, physicians and legal scholars which followed the publication of these incidents focused attention on the whole problem of fetal euthanasia. No one questioned Mrs. Finkbine's human motives, but there was widespread discussion as to her responsibilities to her child, the legal responsibilities of her physicians, and the moral stature of the laws which govern this kind of situation.

The drug taken by Mrs. Finkbine, thalidomide, is only one example of an exterior cause of congenital defects. There are other chemical compounds which can cause fetal defects; discovering and preventing the use of such compounds is of major concern to the Federal Food and Drug Administration. Another factor which can cause serious mental or physical defects in an unborn child is maternal infection. Among the more common infections of the mother causing fetal defects are German Measles, syphilis, malaria and polio. Of these infections German Measles has attracted the most attention in the United States. The exact rate of congenital defects attributable to German Measles is disputed, but a study of the 1964 epidemic in Indiana revealed that about 15% of the women who were infected in the first three months of pregnancy bore children with serious abnormalities of the eyes, ears or heart. Exposure of a pregnant woman to extensive radiation, such as might occur in therapeutic X-ray treatment for cancer of the cervix, is another cause of fetal malformation. Physical trauma on a pregnant woman can harm the child. If, for example, a physical blow on the mother in an auto accident should harm the placenta a decline in the flow of oxygen to the unborn child may possibly result in serious damage to the brain.

In addition to these and other environmental causes of defects in unborn children, there are hereditary factors to be considered. The sex chromosome abnormality XYY may create a predisposition to anti-social violence; in October, 1968, Edward Hannell of Australia, an accused murderer, was allowed to introduce evidence of this chromosomal abnormality at his trial to establish a defense of insanity. Thus, Hannell's alleged predisposition to crime existed while he was still a fetus because it was iherent in his genetic make-up!

As man's knowledge of the causes and statistical chances of serious fetal mental or physical defect increases, eugenic abortion seems to become a more practical tool for preventing human misery and protecting society against misfits. Physicians still must largely make educated guesses as to the condition of the fetus in early pregnancy. However, it is probable that in the not too distant future medical science will have the tools and techniques to probe the mysteries of the womb.

Already, the use of amniocentesis has shown great promise in this direction. A hollow needle is pushed through the abdominal wall and into the womb. A sample of the amniotic fluid is then withdrawn. The fluid contains pigments and cells from the lungs, bladder and skin of the child. When the cells and pigments are examined some fetal abnormalities can be determined. For example, RH incompatibility can be ascertained. Since the sex of the child can be discovered by amniocentesis, predictions of hemophilia in the offspring of parents with a history of the disease can be accurately made if the child is a male. In Sweden, several abortions of unborn children diagnosed as hemophiliacs have already been performed. Amniocentesis will also enable researchers to detect chromosomal aberrations such as those which cause Mongolian Idiocy. Already radiographic and radioisotopic techniques are used to determine if placental placement is harmful to the physical development of the child. Electrocardiograms of the fetal heart can be taken.

Opponents of eugenic abortion frequently argue that it is impractical because it involves guesswork which causes a tremendous destruction of non-defective unborn children. Today there is still a wastage of healthy fetal life in eugenic abortion. But this argument has a rapidly decreasing validity. The techniques for examining the fetus are only a beginning; the new science of fetology will no doubt make the life of the womb more and more accessible to medical knowledge. Knowledge of fetal defects will in the future be not the product of statistical estimates but of direct observation.

However, advances in fetology do not necessarily mean that abortion is the most practical solution to the problem of serious congenital defects. If a needle can penetrate the womb to determine if there is an RH incompatibility between the blood of the mother and that of the child, can not a needle also bring life-saving blood transfusions to the child? Amniocentesis created the opportunity for the intrauterine blood transfusion. In the future the science of fetology will destroy the threat of RH incompatibility. It will be destroyed not by killing every child endangered by the condition but by creating the opportunity for these children to develop normally. Can there be any doubt of which approach is both morally superior and most practical?

Intrauterine blood transfusions are, of course, isolated examples of techniques for preventing fetal defects. The all-too frequent incidence of congenital defects indicates that such examples are rare. But these examples point up a most serious defect in eugenic abortion. Abortion seems an "easy" solution to the problem of congenital defects, but "easy" answers to human problems have a way of having hidden costs. The cost of widespread use of eugenic abortion would be a forfeiture of serious attempts to prevent or cure congenital defects in the early stages of pregnancy. A future in which a pregnant woman can be aided to bring every child she conceives to full term free of serious defects seems both more humane and more practical than simply killing defective children in the womb. Can there be any doubt but that the primary motivation into research on fetal defects is provided by the desire of practicing physicians to prevent congenital defects in the children conceived by their patients? Only if that motivation is destroyed does the "easy" solution of eugenic abortion appear practical. Paradoxically, the practice of eugenic abortion would dull and utimately destroy that motivation.

A British medical researcher has aptly phrased a question which shows the impracticability of eugenic abortion: "is it seriously asserted that our message to those with congenital defects is that they would have been better off unborn?"[3] Does not eugenic abortion cause man to minimize his interest in potential techniques such as pre-natal surgery which could improve the quality of fetal life? Does not eugenic abortion require man to think the unthinkable: that it is better to destroy life than to improve it?

Eugenic Abortion and Christian Morality

Eugenic abortion, while raising some of the moral problems inherent in other forms of abortion, presents a deeply troubling question about the value of human life. To some, eugenic considerations justify the termination of pregnancy:

> if the child will be born mentally defective, or otherwise incapable of a normal life . . . which cannot be reasonably compensated for, it is preferable that its incipient life be nipped in the bud.[4]

Joseph Fletcher of the Episcopal Theological School has argued that seriously defective life should be destroyed in the womb while it is still lacking in freedom, knowledge and the power of service.

There are others who believe that eugenic abortion is the

---

[3] *British Medical Journal*, No. 5416, p. 1076.
[4] 17 Western Reserve Univ. Law Rev. 371.

least justifiable form of abortion. This is the position of the Church Assembly Board of Social Responsibility of the Church of England. While accepting other indications for abortion the Board rejects "fetal euthanasia" even if the physician is certain that the child is defective: "To kill the deformed and unconsulted . . . on the ground that it was in their own interest for them to be killed, would be as unethical as it would be socially dangerous." Most Christians would agree that it is desirable to prevent seriously defective human beings from coming into existence. Pope Pius XII listed "eugenic considerations" among the good reasons for practicing conception control. But to improve life by destroying already existing life is to contradict the reverence for human beings which is a touchstone of Judeo-Christian morality. This is why the Fathers of the Second Vatican condemned both euthanasia and abortion with other wrongs which are opposed to life:

> In our times a special obligation binds us to make ourselves the neighbor of absolutely every person, and of actively helping him when he comes across our path, whether he be an old person abandoned by all, a foreign laborer unjustly looked down upon, a refugee, a child born of an unlawful union and wrongly suffering for a sin he did not commit, or a hungry person who disturbs our conscience by recalling the voice of the Lord: "As long as you did it for one of these, the least of my brethren, you did it for me (Mt 25:40).
>
> Furthermore, whatever is opposed to life itself, such as any type of murder, genocide, abortion, euthanasia, or willful self-destruction, whatever violates the integrity of the human person, such as mutilation, torments inflicted on body or mind, attempts to coerce the will itself; whatever insults human dignity, such as sub-human living conditions, arbitrary imprisonment, deportation, slavery, prostitution, the selling of women and children; as well as disgraceful working conditions, where men are treated as mere tools for profit, rather than as free responsible persons; all these things and others or their like are infamies indeed. They poison human society, but they do more harm to those who practice them than those who suffer from the injury. Moreover, they are a supreme dishonor to the Creator (*Church in the Modern World* § 27).

Of course, the growth of the community-orientated conscience appreciates the need to consider the commonweal when discussing congenital defects. The General Board of the National Council of Churches has observed that the "ethical complexities" of eugenic abortion "need additional study by Christian scholars." That some dilemma confronts the community-conscious believer is apparent. Should his reverence for the common good cause him to approve the destruction of defective fetal life in order to improve the social and/or genetic condition of humanity? Or is the life of the unborn child so sanctified in God's image that even though it is defective its further development cannot be prevented? In this, Karl Barth spoke for the Christian conscience when he observed that to destroy a fetus is to exert the power of decreeing the death of a fellow man.

From a social viewpoint children with grave mental or physical defects may be a real community problem, but this does not justify the killing of defectives. For this reason the Executive Committee of the American Lutheran Church in 1963 approved abortion when necessary to the life or health of the mother, but rejected eugenic abortion. The committee compared this form of abortion to Nazi euthanasia of social defectives. The proper moral response to human defect is not death and destruction, but rather cure and prevention.

Modern morality is preeminently practical. While it rejects eugenic abortion it will not be satisfied with the rejection. To be moral is to act as Christ when presented with human suffering; simply rejecting a solution as immoral while ignoring the problem is not typical of twentieth-century Christian morality.

The continued presence of congenital defects in human life is a condition the Christian conscience cannot witness without being disturbed. As long as babies are born with damaged brains, twisted spines, sightless eyes, stumps for limbs or mentally retarded, no Jew or Christian can be satisfied with merely rejecting eugenic abortion. It is no more moral to

ignore human suffering than it is to kill the sufferer. Christ
condemns the priest who passed by the man lying on the
road to Jericho even more than he condemns the robbers
who beat him.

The Legalization of Eugenic Abortion

The technique of expelling an unborn child from the womb
before he is viable is perhaps most frequently discussed from
the viewpoint of the civil law. There are many who believe
that the advent of eugenic abortion requires serious re-exami-
nation of the proposition that every human life is inviolable
in the eyes of the law. Abortion of defective unborn children
is permitted in a few nations of the world, but is forbidden
in most. Proposals to legalize the practice have served as the
catalyst toward making eugenic abortion the focal point for
consideration of the legal rights of defective life. Discussion
of eugenic abortion inevitably leads to consideration of legalized infanticide and adult euthanasia.

Merely because the Christian considers eugenic abortion
immoral does not settle his attitude toward the legalization
of the practice. *The Declaration on Religious Freedom* issued
by the Second Vatican Council clearly implies that a Christian
should not impose his beliefs on others through the state.
Certainly a Christian in a pluralist society committed to
government impartiality in religion should not impose his
moral convictions on that society. Of course, this general
proposition does not answer the concrete question of whether
the Christian citizen should approve or disapprove of the
legalization of eugenic abortion. If the Christian believes that
eugenic abortion is a wrongful denial of human rights and/or
destructive of the values of the commonweal, it is obvious
that he can in good conscience support prohibition of the
practice. No doubt the Judeo-Christian ethic has influenced
the formation of his opinion, but it would be nonsense to say
that he is imposing his beliefs on others in these circumstances. It is also true that the believer who is convinced

that eugenic abortion is immoral may support its legalization if he believes that the practice is desirable as a matter of public policy. The current debate over the legalization of eugenic abortion has found committed Christians on both sides of the proposition.

In 1938, Sweden became the first nation of the world to permit legal abortion when "there is reason to believe that the mother or the father of the expected child will, as a result of hereditary predisposition, transmit to their offspring insanity, mental deficiency, serious disease or other defects." Defects due to environmental causes such as drugs were later included in the law. Eugenic abortions are permitted only if the Royal Medical Board is convinced that the defective condition exists and gives its approval. Denmark legalized eugenic abortion in the same year. Pregnancy can be terminated "if there is a manifest danger that, because of hereditary predisposition or defect originating at the fetal stage, the child would suffer from insanity, mental deficiency or serious and incurable abnormality or physical disease." The Institute of Human Genetics at the University of Copenhagen maintains hereditary records of each Danish family, and these records are consulted in determining the desirability of eugenic abortion. In both Sweden and Denmark eugenic abortion constitutes a relatively small proportion of legal abortions. The German Democratic Republic allows abortion when "one parent is afflicted with a severe hereditary disease." Norway, Finland, and Switzerland also expressly recognize limited forms of eugenic abortion. Abortions can be obtained by request for any reason in the Soviet Union, People's Republic of China, Japan, Czechoslovakia, Poland and Hungary; the incidence of eugenic abortion in these countries is not known.

In the United States the legal status of eugenic abortion is vague. Only in Colorado and North Carolina is the practice clearly legal, and then only when there is a strong probability that the child will be born with substantial or permanent physical or mental defects. The statutes of most states do not include eugenic indications in the grounds for legal abortions.

However, some physicians do perform such abortions in hospitals under a theory of "preserving the (mental) life or health of the mother." In 1967, the House of Delegates of the American Medical Association, which had previously condemned eugenic abortion as unethical, resolved that a termination of pregnancy on such grounds was not unethical. That many physicians consider eugenic abortions both legal and ethical was apparent during the epidemic of German Measles of 1964–65. Since 1941, it had been known that when a pregnant woman experiences this infection in the early months there is a marked increase in the possibility of physical abnormality in the child. There is evidence that many physicians, with hospital authorization, performed eugenic abortions during the epidemic. Eugenic abortions constitute a substantial part of hospital-approved abortions even when there is no German measles epidemic. Studies have shown that between 9% and 28% of such abortions were done because of fears that the child would be defective.

These practices, the ambiguity of the law, and proposals for legalization raise difficult questions. Should a mother have a legal right to decide that her child would not want to continue living with serious defects? Is the dependence of the child on the mother during pregnancy the basis for such a right? Why does a mother not have the same right in relation to a totally dependent and defective infant after birth? Does an unborn child have a right to life so that society cannot permit anyone to kill him because he is defective? Is the good of the community better served by the mother who aborts or the mother who bears her child and attempts to make him a good citizen in spite of his blindness or his mental deficiency? The American conscience has not yet clearly embodied an answer to these questions in its law.

Should the law permit a pregnant woman and her physician to determine whether an unborn child will be destroyed because it is defective? The Model Penal Code, a criminal law advocated by a private group, proposes that eugenic abortion should be legal. The Code would allow a termination of pregnancy if "there is substantial risk . . . that the child would be born with grave physical or mental defect." Advocates of this position premise their arguments on the good of the child as well as of the mother and society:

> Another type of social problem arises . . . when the odds are good that the fetus has been deformed by some disease, drug, or unnatural occurrence. Many families will be over-burdened financially to provide medical care for these de-formed babies, to say nothing of the heartbreak of the parents and the psychological impact on the children themselves as they grow older and attempt to take their place in society . . . Those children born congenitally deformed or mentally ill as a result of our poorly written abortion laws may be a great financial burden, especially if they need institutional care for prolonged periods. To the more practical minded euthanasia would probably be an answer for this problem.[5]

Even some persons who oppose legalization of infant or adult euthanasia support legalization of eugenic abortion. The acceptance of this position requires a belief that an unborn child is not a person entitled to legal rights and civil protec-tion. Such a position encounters tremendous problems in American legal thought. Obviously no one, certainly not the lawyer, can establish with absolute certainty at what stage in its development a human being becomes a "person." The biologist may define the person in terms of genetic make-up, the social scientist in terms of social development, the phi-losopher in terms of intellectual capacity, the theologian in terms of salvational potential. The lawyer must admit that he can not provide a perfect test for human personality, but he has many tests for the presence of legal personality. Just as the law insists that an idiot, a blind man or a criminal is a person whose rights must be respected, it likewise indicates that an unborn child is the depository of fundamental civil rights. Down through the centuries Anglo-American judges have consistantly protected the rights of unborn children.

Some simple examples will illustrate the incompatibility

---

[5] 37 Temple Law Quarterly 178–179 (1964).

between eugenic abortion and the Anglo-American legal tradition. It is well established that a child who is injured while in his mother's womb can after his birth sue the person who wrongfully injured him. For example, in 1960, the Supreme Court of Pennsylvania allowed a suit by a child who had been injured in the first month of pregnancy with the explanation that "medical authorities have long since recognized that a child is in existence from the moment of its conception."[6] Judge Bergen of the New York Court of Appeals has stressed the separability of the child from its mother in explaining why a child injured in the womb can sue:

> Legal separability should begin where there is biological separability. We know something more of the actual process of conception and fetal development now than when the common law cases were decided; and what we know makes it possible to demonstrate clearly that separability begins at conception. The mother's biological contribution from conception on is nourishment and protection, but the fetus has become a separate organism and remains so throughout life. That it may not live if its protection and nourishment are cut off earlier than the viable stage . . . is not to destroy separability; it is rather to describe the conditions under which life will not continue.[7]

However, this right of the child to sue the person who has injured him is subject to being destroyed if he dies before birth.[8] If eugenic abortion were legal a child who had been seriously injured in the womb could be killed by the decision of the mother and some physicians (even if one of these persons was the wrongdoer). Thus, private persons would be empowered by the state to destroy the child's right to sue. Students of constitutional law will immediately recognize that the child is being deprived of property (the lawsuit) under state authorization without due process of law. That he is

---

[6] Sinkler v. Kneale 164 A.2d 93 (1960).

[7] Kelly v. Gregory 125 N.Y.S. 2d 696 (1953)

[8] If his death is caused by a wrongdoer, the heirs of the fetus can sue in most states.

also being deprived of his life without due process is even more apparent and legally objectionable.

For centuries the common law has recognized the right of a fetus to inherit or take by will if his ancestor should die while the child is still in the womb. For example, when a Mrs. Wells died on May 22, 1922, she left a will providing a trust fund for her "grandchildren living at the time of my decease." At this date a grandchild, Elizabeth Davis, had been in the womb of her mother for about 21 days. The New York Court held that Elizabeth "was and is a living child for all purposes pertaining to her property rights" at the time of the grandmother's death.[9] If, however, the child is not born alive the property will pass to other persons. Judge George Fiedler has posed the obvious inconsistancy between these property rights of the child and eugenic abortion:

> An unborn child is capable of taking a legacy or an in- heritance, subject to being divested if not born alive. Would the mental health or mental well-being of parents who might succeed to the inheritance be considered by the doctors or hospital abortion board if the parents could show that they would be happier, and their mental health better, if their shares were enlarged by the "termination of the pregnancy"?
>
> The Fifth Amendment and the Fourteenth Amendment provide that no person shall be deprived of property without due process of law, and no State may deny any person the equal protection of its laws. When may a panel of doctors or a hospital abortion board deprive an unborn child of his property or property rights?[10]

The Anglo-American legal tradition has always prided itself on its protection of the weak, the poor and innocent from the overreaching hand of the more powerful. To those who argue that the law should enable physicians to kill the de- formed child merely because he has not yet passed through the stage of birth, Judge Dempsey of Illinois has provided an answer:

---

[9] In Re Well's Will, 221 N.Y. Supp. 417 (1927)
[10] Letter to *America*, Jan. 20, 1968, p. 81.

How can the law distinguish the day-to-day development of
life? If there is human life, proved by subsequent birth, then
that life has the same rights at the time of conception as it has
at any time thereafter.[11]

To cut and scrape a developed child from its mother's
womb because it is physically or mentally defective is incompatible with the historic tradition of equal protection so
fundamental to American constitutional law. For decades this
law has been evolving a refined and highly moral construct
of the innate value of human life. Regardless of a person's
physical, mental or social inadequacies, before the law each
is entitled to equal protection. Simply because an adult might
consider a child's life unworthy, there is no reason for the
state to permit that child's destruction. The distinguished
legal scholar Norman St. John Stevas has described the variance between eugenic abortion and the attitude of the law:

It [eugenic abortion] presupposes that one human being
can make a judgment about another as to whether that other's
life is worth living and enforce it, a power that has never
been conferred by Anglo-American law. It confers a license
to kill and one with no clear limiting terms. To one person
life without sight will appear unbearable; to another the
absence of arms, to another the lack of legs. Instead of a clear
standard of law there is substituted the subjective canon of
personal taste.[12]

If a Christian citizen in good conscience believes that eugenic abortion is an infringement on fundamental human and
legal rights, he should oppose legalization of the practice.
Some people will accuse him of "imposing his beliefs on
others," but he speaks from the framework of his nation's
legal traditions.

Both the Christian and the citizen should be aware that
congenital defects can be overcome by means which do not
have the social, moral and legal faults of eugenic abortion.
These and other means must be carefully considered and sup-

---

11 Zepeda v. Zepeda, 190 N.E. 2d 849 (1963).
12 "Abortion Laws," *Commonweal* Nov. 11, 1966, p. 163.

ported. It is as morally inferior to ignore human suffering as it is to seek the death of the persons suffering. What are some of the means by which congenital defects can be eliminated or at least minimized?

One thoughtful proposal is compulsory premarital genetic counselling. Neither the canon nor state law of marriage requires such counselling prior to marriage. The effectiveness of voluntary genetic counselling has been demonstrated. The constitutionality of certain forms of compulsory premarital testing, such as blood tests or physical examinations, has been determined by the courts. Canon law requires premarital counselling on the meaning of the sacrament. Should not the law require a couple contemplating marriage to secure advice as to the probable consequences of their mating for offspring? Of course, neither the law of the state nor that of the church can forbid a couple to marry on eugenic grounds without denying the freedom to marry proclaimed by the United States Supreme Court: "The freedom to marry has long been recognized as one of the vital personal rights essential to the orderly pursuit of happiness by free men."[13] Morally, the law should not withhold the freedom to marry from even the eugenically unfit. But every couple should be given the eugenic information they need to appreciate reasonably the effects their union will have on their children.

Lack of proper pre-natal care is a major cause of fetal defect. The good of the commonweal, as well as of the individual child, demands that each pregnant woman should have access to expert pre-natal care. Practically, this means that such care must be made a matter of public health.

Conception control information should also be available to the public from governmental sources. This should include advice on the use of conception control techniques for eugenic purposes. However, the conscience of every couple seeking such advice must be respected. In no case should the government be permitted to pressure a couple into the practice of

---

[13] Loving v. Virginia 388 U.S. 1 (1967).

conception control. Such a practice would be as unjustifiable an intrusion into marital privacy as was the Connecticut practice of outlawing contraceptives which was denounced by the Supreme Court in 1965:

> (Justice Douglas): The present case . . . concerns a relationship lying within the zone of privacy created by fundamental constitutional guarantees. And it concerns a law which, in forbidding the use of contraceptives . . . seeks to achieve its goals by means of having a maximum destructive impact upon that relationship. (Justice Goldberg): Surely the Government, absent a showing of compelling subordinating state interest, could not decree that all husbands and wives must be sterilized after two children have been born . . . if upon a showing of a slender basis of rationality, a law outlawing voluntary birth control is valid, then, by the same reasoning, a law requiring compulsory birth control would also seem to be valid.[14]

While there has been growing interest in congenital defects in recent years, many types of defects remain obscure and untreated. For example, fewer than a dozen physicians in the United States specialize in the care and training of Mongolian Idiots. Since it has been shown that such children can develop excellent social-familial relations and some adequate life skills if given loving care and professional attention, this lack of medical interest is most unjustifiable. How many church-related medical facilities have programs of research in congenital defects? The lack of such programs shows an absence of Christ-like concern on the part of both the institutional church and the medical profession.

One area of the law which has been sadly deficient is that governing adoption. Children with serious defects are often considered unadoptable. Even when there is no state statute inhibiting the adoption of seriously defective children, many judges are reluctant to decree an adoption when a child is seriously handicapped. Even when a couple desires to adopt a defective infant the suspicions of agencies, courts, friends

---

14 Griswold v. Connecticut 381 U.S. 479 (1965)

and neighbors often are detriment factors. When man most needed a father "God sent his Son, born of a woman . . . to enable us to be adopted as sons" (Gal 4:4–5). The Christian's reflections on divine sonship should reveal to him that adoption of the neediest child is an act of special greatness. The institutional church has failed to proclaim this scripture-based truth. Sadly, Christian institutions fail to promote adoption of congenitally defective children as much as the law ignores it.

Our society must recognize that the parent who spends years educating a physically or mentally defective child is giving a great service to the community. History records the deeds of many men who suffered substantial congenital defects of the mind and body. Beethoven, Godfried Mind, Michelangelo, Lord Byron, Authur Kavanaugh and others like them have enriched the race. The congenitally defective child may not make such a contribution, but if his parents successfully educate him to be a worthy and useful citizen the community benefits from their considerable effort. Should not such parents receive some kind of financial assistance from the commonweal if their child's defect is of the type which requires expensive help?

In rejecting eugenic abortion as a solution to the problem of congenital defects the Christian cannot be smug. He is under an obligation to provide alternatives to eugenic abortion. The words of St. John should require him to keep the agony of congenitally defective children in the forefront of his concerns:

> If a man who was rich enough in this world's good saw that one of his brothers was in need, but closed his heart to him, how could the love of God be living in him? My children, our love is not to be just words or mere talk, but something real and active, only by this can we be certain that we are the children of truth . . . Whoever loves the Father that begot him loves the child whom he also begets (John 3: 17–19; 5:1).

CHAPTER III

DEATH AND THE QUALITY OF LIFE

Should Society Kill the Criminal?

As a law professor interested in penology I was invited by officials of the Massachusetts Correctional System to tour the state prison for men. After seeing the many sides of prison life, including the excellent programs for prisoner rehabilitation, I was preparing to leave when my guide asked me if I would like to view the death chamber. We walked across a sunny opening and into a small cold room. The guard left for a few minutes to take care of another matter. Since this new prison had been erected no one had been put to death here, but the electric chair which had been brought here from the old prison had been the instrument of death for many men. I sat down in the old wooden chair. In front of me was a mirror. "Why would they want a mirror in front of him?" I asked myself. It was a two-way mirror; behind it stand the "official witnesses" who view the killing on behalf of "the people." I looked up at the pipe which ran up the back of the chair to the head of the person being killed. Through that pipe had come the electrical current which killed Sacco and Vanzetti as they sat on this chair. As the guard returned to the room I thought to myself: "Is Massachusetts a better place to live in today because it killed Sacco and Vanzetti?"

For the executed criminal there is no redemption. If capital punishment has any value it must be some benefit for society. It has been shown that capital punishment has no value as a deterrent to violent crimes of passion. It may be that many members of society get satisfaction from the realization that murderers and rapists can be burned to death by electrical power. Perhaps the electric chair, the firing squad and the gas chamber are society's security blankets. Or, in the final analysis, capital punishment may simply be society's ultimate retribution against those who have violated its laws.

It is sometimes said that capital punishment should be abolished because there is danger that an innocent man may be killed. The danger is slight, but it does exist. The example of one state, Massachusetts, illustrates the danger. Cero Gangi was convicted of murder and sentenced to die in the electric chair in 1928. On the day set for execution a witness identified another man as the murderer. Gangi was reprieved at the last minute. He was subsequently re-tried and found not guilty. In 1934 two men went on trial for murder in Salem, Massachusetts. The defendants were identified as the murderers by eight different eyewitnesses. Before the case went to the jury three other men confessed to the crime and admitted that the two defendants were in no way involved. More recently, Santos Rodriguez was held in a Massachusetts prison for three years after being convicted of murder; he was discovered to be innocent of the crime and released in 1957. Many investigators believe that the Commonwealth took the lives of two innocent men when it executed Sacco and Vanzetti.

There are some who believe that capital punishment is a dead issue. Few executions have taken place in the United States in recent years. But the very existence of capital punishment is of concern to the moralist. The lawyer is very much aware of the fact that the death penalty has continuing effects on the administration of criminal justice. When the public temper is aroused in a fit of emotion because of some horrible crime, there is widespread demand for bloodletting against the first suspect apprehended. When hundreds of men are sentenced to die each year and two or three are actually executed public cynicism about criminal courts and American penology is deepened. The existence of capital punishment makes the administration of criminal justice much more complicated than it needs to be. Judges and lawyers realize that because of the death penalty, trial and appellate courts spend much more time and money with capital cases than can be justified in terms of the court's entire docket. In states with capital punishment the selection of a jury in capital cases is frequently much more time consuming even though there is little chance that the punishment will be imposed. A great number of respected penologists, including the wardens of leading prisons and jails, are convinced that the existence of the death penalty is a deterrent to effective penal reform.

The pragmatic arguments for and against capital punishment are inconclusive. J. Edgar Hoover spoke from decades of experience in law enforcement when he said that the death penalty protects the lives of policemen. But statistics indicate no higher rate of police deaths in non-capital punishment states. The opponents of capital punishment argue that it is a brutal and brutalizing form of punishment. To this Jacques Barzun has replied that the confinement, degradation, sexual promiscuity and utter monotony of imprisonment constitute a much more inhumane and brutal punishment than death. Back and forth go the arguments. Some religious persons may agree with Reinhold Niebuhr that the desirability of capital punishment should be determined solely by its social results, but the great majority of American Christian denominations have advocated its repeal on the grounds that the practice is incompatible with Christ's message of redemption. However, most Catholic moralists teach that the state has the power to execute a criminal.

I believe that capital punishment should have no place in twentieth-century America. In *Pacem in Terris* Pope John called for a legal structure which corresponds to both the moral and political development of the community. In the evolution of the moral consciousness and political structures of modern man one can detect a noticeable movement away from killing as a solution to human problems. Only the movements to retain capital punishment and legalize abortion run counter to this evolutionary development. As man's spirit evolves he realizes that killing is simply not a civilized solution to his problems. Man has dedicated himself to the elimination of post-natal abortifacients such as war; he must now reject completely the proposition that human life can be made better by eliminating unwanted persons. There is good reason to believe that the United States Supreme Court will find the whole process of capital punishment to be a cruel and unusual punishment at some future date. It recently ruled that a prospective juror cannot be kept off a jury simply because he does not believe in capital punishment. It is a process in which a condemned man is typically held under threat of death for many years before he is executed or reprieved. Capital punishment was obviously not considered a cruel and unusual punishment when the Constitution was written. But man's moral sensibilities have evolved since the eighteenth century. A most astute observer of moral evolution, Ignace Lepp, has rightly suggested that modern morality ought to reject capital punishment simply because of its respect for the character of human existence.

The Moral and Legal Implications of Surgical Transplants

In 1904 Alexis Carrel and Charles Guthrie of the University of Chicago transplanted a kidney from one dog to another. The surgical technique of organ transplantation had been created. Carrel won the Nobel prize in 1912 for his work, but it was not until 1954 that a successful transplant of a human kidney was accomplished in Boston. As the ability of medical science to reduce the danger of organ rejection developed, the number of human kidney transplants increased in the early sixties. In recent years we have also witnessed successful transplants of human livers, pancreases, duodenums, lung lobes and hearts. Scientists believe that in the near future transplants of spleens, brains and entire heads will be feasible. All forms of organ transplants, even kidney transplants, are still largely experimental. Patient treatment is a factor in these operations, but a subordinate one in the opinion of many medical authorities. It is important to weigh this fact in considering the morality and legality of organ transplants. Is the need for trial and error experiment with organ transplantation sufficient justification for practices now occuring in some leading medical centers?

The first moralists to consider organ transplants did so from the viewpoint of the donor. To a great degree these early studies were colored by the horrible stories of Nazi medical experimentation which had shocked the conscience of mankind. Catholic theologians were also influenced by papal teachings on mutilation which had been developed in the framework of the debate over conception control. Fearful that social pressures on the donor would not make consent really free, some moralists condemned transplants from living donors. Catholic moralists who accepted the principle of totality, i.e., that mutilation is not moral unless necessary or useful to the body as a whole, tended to condemn organ transplants as harmful to the body of the donor. However, in the mid-nineteen forties two American Catholic theologians proposed that a man who sacrifices part of his own body for the good of his neighbor is doing a most Christian act. Bert J. Cunningham and Gerald Kelly suggested that since all men were one in Christ, the transfer of organs from one to another as an act of love is an act of high moral quality. The lavish praise of blood-donors by Pope Pius XII made many Catholics realize that a man who shares part of his body with his neighbor in need acts as Christ did when he gave himself. There no longer appears to be any substantial theological opposition to organ transplantation from a donor who knowingly and freely consents to give an organ on which he is not himself absolutely dependent.

One of the most troublesome aspects of current transplant surgery is that in a number of cases the donor is incapable of personally consenting. The Donation of Organic Tissue Acts passed by a number of states do not solve many of the legal issues, and American society has not yet evolved a clear set of moral premises to guide the persons involved in such operations. In heart transplants, for example, an unconscious patient who is judged to be dying may be chosen as a donor. The patient's closest relatives will be told of his "terminal" condition. If they consent to the operation, judgments as to treatment of the dying patient will then probably be colored by the knowledge that his heart will shortly be used for the transplant.

When the patient is declared dead, every effort will be made to revive or retain vital activities in the heart until the transplant takes place. During this period the brain of the donor will continue to function; the presence of such brain activity is accepted by most medical authorities as a sign that death has not yet happened. When the heart is taken from the patient, is it being cut from a cadaver or the body of a living person? Was the consent given by the relatives to allow the physicians to take the heart of a dead man or the heart of a living man? If it is the former the consent is both moral and legally effective; if it is the latter the consent is immoral and does not excuse the physicians from liability for homicide under the law. A Swedish physician who removed a kidney from a young man dying of a fatal brain injury was accused of murder; the situation of the heart surgeon is much more difficult.

In a pioneering heart transplant the donor was a young woman who had sustained a serious head injury. The neurologist judged the injury to be lethal. The young woman's relatives consented to the transplant. The equipment being used to sustain the woman's life was shut off. A few minutes later the heart was removed and transplanted to a man suffering from serious heart disease. A pathologist subsequently judged that the head injury suffered by the donor had not necessarily been lethal. This story should indicate the essentially moral considerations which must affect the physicians' judgments and choices in these cases. The law might intervene with a requirement that all decisions affecting the treatment of the donor be made by physicians who are not on the transplanting team (a practice which has been followed in the heart transplants), but this would provide little effective protection to the donor. Certainly the law cannot substitute formulas for the judgment of the physicians, since the practice of medicine involves the exercise of professional but personal judgments by the physician. Medical judgments about the probability of recovery by a potential donor are obviously highly fallible.

Even in a case in which every physician would predict death, can a vital organ be taken from the body of a man whose life functions are continuing? A moral theologian or criminal court jury might judge the physician who took the heart from a body which still showed signs of life to be guilty of murder; others might believe that he merely took the organ while it still could be used for a transplant. If the physician waited until the brain waves were perfectly flat then the heart might be useless. The fundamental problem here is that there exists no universally accepted definition of death in medicine or law. The International Commission of Medical Ethics defines death as the absence of brain activity. But death is sometimes defined in terms of the absence of pulmonary or heart activity. Should the law step in with a single definition? Would such a definition best be expressed as the absence of any vital activity, or would some less demanding definition be sufficient to protect the moral and legal rights of all concerned? Might it be even more desirable for death to be defined as a process rather than an event? Would a statement of death as a process of deterioration in which there is no reasonable hope of survival satisfy the moralist and the Anglo-American legal tradition of respect for life?

There has been a great, and understandable, reluctance on the part of everyone concerned to answer these questions. Some moralists have said that death is a medical question which the physician can define from a framework of his experience. Others have urged the law to define death from the framework of its social concern. Since law is the means by which society balances conflicting interests, is not some legal definition of death required to balance the diverse interests of the donor, the recipient, the physician and the community? Some commentators believe that a legal definition would inhibit progress in surgical transplant experimentation. This entire problem may be eliminated in the future when mechanical or animal organs are made available for transplantation into humans, but at present it constitutes an extremely difficult moral and legal problem for medical science.

What limits can be assigned to the power of the state in using the bodies of its deceased citizens as a source of organ supply should an adequate definition of death be agreed on? May the legislature morally provide that bodies may be used to obtain organs, even if the deceased or his next-of-kin did not consent to removal of the organs? While the law has always insisted that no one has a property right in a dead body, law courts have sometimes protected the feelings and emotions of living persons who fear that a misuse is being made of a loved-one's body. However, there would seem to be no constitutional objection to compulsory taking, storage, and transplantation of parts of a dead body. Moral theologians could not object to such legislation on the basis of any traditional principles of their science. The state should be able to provide for the good of its citizens by reasonable and dignified use of dead bodies.

The legal relationship between the donor and recipient of a transplanted organ, and between the physician and the parties, is far from clear today. Carl Sirianni had been subjected to medical treatment which harmed rather then helped him. As a result of this harm Carl required a kidney transplant in order to survive. Mrs. Sirianni, Carl's mother, volunteered to donate one of her kidneys. As a result of the transplant Carl survived. Later, Carl sued the physicians for medical malpractice. This suit was settled out of court, with Carl receiving a sizable amount of money. Mrs. Sirianni then sued the physicians, saying that the removal of her kidney constituted an injury to her. The New York court dismissed her suit. Judge Ward wrote:

> the complaint alleges that the defendants negligently re-
> moved all of the kidney tissue of one Carl Sirianni during . . .
> a surgical procedure conducted by and participated in by the
> defendants as physicians and surgeons . . . stripped of emo-
> tionalism the issue here is, does a cause of action exist in favor
> of a donor of a human organ against defendants who removed
> vital human organs from the donee in a negligent manner?
> . . . The premeditated, knowledgeable and purposeful act of
> this plaintiff (Mrs. Sirianni) in donating one of her kidneys
> to preserve the life of her son did not extend or reactivate the
> consummated negligence of these defendants. The conduct of
> (Mrs. Sirianni) . . . is a clear, defined, independent, inter-
> vening act with full knowledge of the consequences. The
> miracle of modern medicine seems now on the threshold of
> successfully transferring many organs from one human body to
> another. The issue raised here may in the future frequently
> find its way into the courts. This issue should be settled. If
> public policy requires that a donor is permitted (to sue) . . .
> under the circumstances here, such cause of action must be
> created, not by judicial fiat, but by legislation.[1]

In the not-too-distant future a surgeon will transplant a human brain or a head from one body to another. Since the brain is generally acknowledged as the center for man's mental, spiritual and artistic powers such a transplant raises difficult problems. Traditionalist theologians, used to defining man in terms of a body-soul distinction, would have enormous specu-lative problems with such an operation. Modern moralists, who reason within a framework of social concern, may find fewer problems with a brain transplant, but they cannot be oblivious to the social difficulties such operations would create. The lawyer, that pragmatic individual who wants to advise his client accurately on how to dispose of his estate on death, can only shake his head in despair at the thought of a brain transplant. Who has survived and who has died? If both the

---

[1] Sirianni v. Anna 285 N.Y.S. 2d 709 (1968).

donor and the recipient have died, does the new being have any interest in the estate of either? Should the donor or the recipient attempt to protect his interests by leaving property to the new being? What is the relationship of this new being to the wife of the donor, or the wife of the recipient? It has been said that because of the ability of science to preserve sperm after the death of a donor for purposes of artificial insemination the law may have to recognize a creature known as the fertile dead man. Brain transplants may require the law to create categories even more fantastic than this. The time to start considering the moral and legal implications of such operations is now.

The Legal and Moral Limits of Medical Experimentation on Human Beings

In 1963 two physicians, Emanuel Mandel and Chester Southam, were engaged in cancer research at the Jewish Chronic Disease Hospital in Brooklyn, New York. Mandel was medical director of the hospital, Southam was a professor at the Cornell University Medical School. As part of an experiment being funded by the United States government and the American Cancer Society the physicians decided to introduce live cancer cells into the bodies of twenty-one patients at the hospital. The physicians believed that the experiment involved no risk for the patients. The patients were not informed of the procedure. Although the patients were weak from other causes, none of them was suffering from cancer. The procedure was in no sense intended as treatment for the patients.

Mandel asked three members of his staff for their opinions. The staff members objected, but Mandel decided to proceed with the experiment. After the experiment the staff members resigned in protest. Because of this protest a hospital grievance committee heard charges against Mandel and Southam. The committee praised the work of the physicians; the hospital's Board of Directors voted to commend them. Because of the publicity surrounding these events, the incident came to the attention of state officials. The New York Board of Regents ruled that Mandel and Southam were guilty of unprofessional conduct. Their licenses to practice medicine were revoked for one year, but this was subsequently modified to one year of probationary status.

It is obvious that research and experimentation on human beings is essential to medical progress. Some of this experimentation must involve risks. But what are the legal and moral limits of such experimentation? At Nuremberg German scientists were condemned because they conducted experiments on human beings without the consent of the subjects of the test. The United States Military Tribunal at Nuremberg stressed that human experimentation can be legally justified only if the patient gives his consent with understanding, freedom, and knowledge of the dangers, inconveniences and length of the experiment. But this requirement of full disclosure and free consent has been widely criticized by some medical experimentors, and I have spoken to some scientists who admit that the requirement of informed consent is widely ignored. The Declaration of Helsinki, a statement of medical ethics accepted by the American Medical Association, permits the physician to obtain consent to experiment without full disclosure when such disclosure would not be "consistent with patient psychology." While no American physician has ever been convicted of homicide in the death of a patient resulting from a treatment-experiment procedure, prosecutions are possible under statutes dealing with homicide or even mayhem or aiding a suicide. Since there is no legislation expressly setting forth the limits of human experimentation, the general laws governing the taking or endangering of human life apply to the scientist as much as to anyone else. The license of a physician is not a license to endanger human life. Of course, the informed consent of the patient will protect the physician from private suits by the patient or his estate under a theory of "assumed risk."

From the viewpoint of Judeo-Christian morality even full

disclosure and free consent would not excuse a medical researcher who conducts a highly dangerous experiment if safer
methods of patient treatment are available. If the experiment
is in no way a treatment for the benefit of the patient, morality
cannot approve it as long as even a minimal danger to human
life or health exists. Even if an experiment is not of itself
morally objectionable, the moralist will insist on full disclosure
and free consent. The late Ignace Lepp, a most perceptive
physician and moral theologian, would even demand full disclosure for a treatment which is largely experimental. Lepp
condemned as unethical and unprofessional those psychiatrists
who induce a patient to accept a treatment of "sleep cure"
when the physician actually intends to use electric shock
treatments.

How widespread is human experimentation? Anyone who
has examined medical journals realizes that it constitutes a
substantial part of medical research. It goes on in every major
hospital in the United States. In some government sponsored
programs, such as space-medicine research, human experimentation is basic to the entire program. It is well known
that drug companies provide samples to physicians for use
on their patients. Information fed by physicians back to the
drug firms provides a major basis for judgment as to the
value of the drugs. Drugs are commonly tested for safety on
persons confined to diverse institutions, including children.
Federal law now requires free informed consent by the patient before a purely experimental drug can be used. But
lobby pressures exerted by the drug industry resulted in an
exception being put into the law. Thus, the administering
physician can dispense with the informed consent of the
patient when he believes that obtaining such consent would
be "contrary to the best interests of such human beings."
Subsequently rulings by the Federal Food and Drug Admin-
istratin require full consent when the drug is being used
primarily for medical research, i.e., not primarily for the
benefit of the patient. The only true safeguard which a
patient has from being used in a human experiment is the

carefully formed conscience and judgment of his physician in adhering to these rules.

The patient will be excused if he questions the protection given by this safeguard. The widely publicized drug MER/29 appeared on the market before current Federal laws and regulations were in effect, but the performance of the medical profession throughout the MER/29 incident raises serious moral questions about the attitude of the profession toward human experimentation. In 1959 William S. Merrill Co., a division of a leading pharmaceutical firm, applied to the F. D. A. for permission to market MER/29. The purpose of the drug was to reduce cholesterol levels and minimize heart attacks. The F. D. A. approved the application, which was supported by reports of both animal and human experiments with the drug over a three year period. The drug was marketed in 1960.

In December, 1961, the Merrill Co. sent a letter to all practicing physicians warning that baldness, dermatitis and cataracts might result from the use of MER/29. In May, 1962, the F. D. A. forbade any further distribution of MER/29 because clinical investigation showed the drug to be unsafe for humans and because Merrill had falsified the reports of experiments which it had given to the F. D. A. For example, cataracts had developed in dogs and rats which had been given MER/29, but this fact had been concealed from the F. D. A. The Merrill Co. and several of its officers and scientists were indicted in December, 1963; the defendants did not contest the prosecutions. The company was fined $80,000 by a federal judge, and the individual defendants were given suspended prison sentences. Merrill has since been sued by hundreds of patients for whom MER/29 had been prescribed. Jury awards have ranged from a few thousand to over a million dollars. Hundreds of claims have been settled by Merrill out of court.

The most disturbing part of this incident has been the attitude of the medical profession. Throughout the country physicians demonstrated a general lack of scientific inquiry by accepting the claims of the drug company about MER/29 at face value. If Merrill and its salesmen said the drug was safe, and the F. D. A. licensed it, this was good enugh for the profession. Some physicians continued to prescribed the drug even after Merrill informed them by letter that MER/29 might cause cataracts, and other physicians prescribed it after some of their patients actually developed cataracts! Patients suing Merrill found great difficulty getting physicians or medical experts to testify in their behalf. However, many physicians testified for the drug company; one medical witness was paid $5,000 per appearance by the company. The director of the Division of Drugs of the American Medical Association testified for Merrill Co. This response of physicians to the MER/29 incident raises serious questions not only about the relationship of the profession to the pharmaceutical industry, but about the moral standards which guide the physician who is using a still-largely-experimental drug on his patients.[2]

The effects of human experimentation on the subject can sometimes be extremely serious. Several years ago Professor Henry Beecher of the Harvard University Medical School cited several dozen medical experiments in which the researchers had violated even the minimal standards of medical ethics governing patient care. In one experiment twenty-three of the patients died. In another several of the subjects contracted rheumatic fever because of the experiment. It is well known that death and serious injury have been caused by drugs which have been marketed in the expectation that widespread usage will determine if they are safe. Can anyone justify the experimentation with early polio vaccines on institutionalized deaf-mutes? Drugs are commonly tested on mental patients who cannot give an informed consent. Morally, such experimentation must stand condemned. Can any civilized standard of law continue to permit such conditions?

---

[2] This account of the MER/29 case is based on the detailed report contained in "The MER/29 Story" by Paul Rheingold, 56 *California Law Review* 116 (1968).

Should Man Permit Himself by Law
to Kill Unborn Children?

In 1936 a physician, Dr. Bourne, was found not guilty of
the crime of abortion by an English jury. Bourne had aborted
a young woman whose child had been conceived as the result
of rape. Bourne's defense was that the life of the mother, in
view of her extreme mental anguish, could be saved only by
aborting the child. In his instructions to the jury Justice
MacNaughten described the attitude of the Anglo-American
law toward the life of the unborn child:

> The law of this land has always held human life to be
> sacred, and the protection that the law gives to human life it
> also extends to the unborn child in the womb. The unborn
> child in the womb must not be destroyed unless the destruc-
> tion of that child is for the purpose of preserving the yet more
> precious life of the mother.[3]

The position of the law that the life of the fetus cannot be
taken unless abortion is clearly necessary to save the life of
the mother is now being challenged. Both lawyers and physicians have proposed moral and pragmatic reasons for increasing the situations in which the law would allow abortion.
Proposals range from legalized abortion in well defined cases,
such as where pregnancy results from rape or incest, to permitting termination of pregnancy at the mother's request.

It is obvious that criminal abortion is a major problem in
the United States. Thousands of women submit to illegal
abortions; perhaps dozens die each year at the hands of
criminal abortionists. However, most of the proposals to
legalize abortion would in no way decrease the incidence of
criminal abortion. Only in extremely rare cases does the
woman who has been made pregnant by rape or incest, or who
fears genetic defects in her child, seek out the criminal abor-

---

[3] Rex v. Bourne 3 All E.R. 615 (K.B. 1938).

tionist. Estimates made by the American Medical Association a few years ago drew the following picture of the typical woman who submits to criminal abortions in the United States: she is white, married, has children, is pregnant by her husband, and is over thirty years of age. It is obvious that such a woman, who is using abortion as a means of birth control, would not be helped by any change in the abortion law short of allowing termination of pregnancy on request. Most of the remaining twenty percent of victims of criminal abortionists are unmarried women who also would not be affected by most of the proposed changes. The condition of these women may constitute a powerful argument for free access to voluntary conception control information and for mandatory programs of sex education at all levels of schooling, but it is no argument for legalizing limited-indication abortion.

If the national debate over the legalization of abortion has had any valuable effect on the development of Judeo Christian moral thought it has been to point up the inconsistency of some allegedly moral positions. Some of the most vocal opposition to abortion legislation came from churchmen who had previously taken stands in favor of military violence. These men demonstrated a rightful reverence for the rights of nascent human life, but advocated policies which approve the taking of mature human life. Is there not a substantial inconsistency in the thought of one who protects the life of the unborn child but approves sending a nineteen-year-old conscript to his death on the battlefield? Is there any difference of moral quality between the act of bombing an "enemy" village and abortion?

Of course, the Christian cannot find any desirable moral qualities in abortion. If the believer has anything to say to the world about killing it is that the sacred life of the human being must not be taken from him with the approval of society. One who accepts the tenets of Judeo-Christian morality must approve the declining use of capital punishment and the growing realization of the absurdity of war. Similiarly, most believers will reject legalized abortion inasmuch as this confers a license to kill unborn children. Such a license is not what we have come to expect in a civilized people. As man evolves toward a higher plane of spiritual development he gradually sheds his desire to solve problems by killing. No doubt the law is correct in allowing abortion when confronted with an absolute choice between the life of the mother and the life of the child, but killing an unborn child to solve social and economic problems is a regression from the civilized standard of modern morality. To permit the killing of a child because his birth would cause social, psychological or economic problems would be to retreat from the historic standards of due process with which the Anglo-American law protects human life from arbitrary treatment. To allow it, would be to weaken one of the finest moral constructs ever created by man.

Some proponents of liberalized legal abortion have engaged in the unfortunate practice of setting up strawmen to advance their arguments. Space does not permit a detailed analysis of these arguments here, but anyone who has participated in the abortion debate will recognize the problem. One example of a strawman will suffice. During the debate which preceded the adoption of the liberalized Colorado law, advocates of this legislation insisted that Catholic morality and canon law at one time permitted abortion. This argument was, of course, completely irrelevant to the question of what kind of legislation would be most suitable for Colorado. It was obviously aimed at upsetting those Catholics who did not understand the evolutionary nature of both morals and law. More importantly, the argument distracted from the real constitutional issues of the debate; if those issues had been examined free from the emotional "religious" argument, the position of the abortion advocates might have been revealed as untenable. The utterly absurd aspect of the entire irrelevant argument over Catholic beliefs and practices is that even the facts of the matter were grossly misrepresented. State legislators who never studied either theology or canon law became instant experts. They ignored the fact that from the earliest days of the church the Christians taught that once a human life comes into existence its being must be respected. In the second century the Christians accepted as a command the principle that "you must not kill a fetus by abortion" (*Epistle of Barnabas*, § 19.5). The first great Latin theologian, Tertullian (a lawyer by profession), explicitly rejected the practice of abortion which was allowed under the Roman law. The first codes of church law contained condemnations of abortion. For example, a decree of the Council of Elvira around 300 A.D. decreed that any Christian who practiced abortion was to be excommunicated from the church. The first code of law in the eastern church condemns abortion without equivocation. St. Basil, the lawgiver of the Greek church, wrote in Letter 188: "Any woman who kills the child in her womb has destroyed a human life." During the middle ages many theologians adopted theories of successive animation. This theory sees life progressing through vegetative and animal stages to the point at which a human soul is "infused." Such a theory is absurd from the viewpoint of modern embryology, but its adoption by writers such as Aquinas would naturally influence the degree of severity with which the medieval church looked at abortion in the early stages of pregnancy. However, moral theology always rejected abortion at any stage. It was not until 1869 that canon law imposed penalties on Catholics who participated in abortions in the early stages of pregnancy. What those who stressed this fact in Colorado failed to understand is that canon law only rarely imposes eccleslesiastical penalties for moral wrongs. For twenty centuries the moral teaching of the church proclaimed that the life of a human being may not be taken from him simply because he is unborn. This fact is in no way relevant to a debate over the state's law of abortion, but no one should misrepresent it.

The Christian and the citizen will want to support programs which are aimed at minimizing the conditions giving rise to a demand for legalized abortion. Certainly a great and wealthy society such as the United States can make greater effort to eliminate the situations which cause a woman to want to kill her child. Some will say: "Why bother; it's easier to legalize abortion." The answer to that was provided by Dr. Joseph DeLee of the University of Chicago, one of the founders of modern obstetrical medicine. At one time DeLee had been a champion of abortion practices. But when he reflected on the worldwide orgy of disrespect for human life in the late thirties and early forties DeLee's attitude underwent a profound change:

> At the present time, when rivers of blood and tears of innocent men, women and children are flowing in most parts of the world, it seems silly to be contending over the right of an unknowable atom of human flesh in the uterus of a woman. No, it is not silly. On the contrary, it is of transcendent importance that there be in this chaotic world one high spot, however small, which is against the deluge of immorality that is sweeping over us. That we in the medical profession hold to the principle of the sacredness of human life and of the right of the individual even though unborn is proof that humanity is not yet lost.[4]

The Human Tendency to Violence

Many observers have noted that America is a violent nation. Riots in the urban areas of the country are but one example of American violence. Criminal attacks on defenseless persons are ignored by citizens who do not want to get "involved." Juvenile authorities are alarmed at the type of violent conduct practiced by substantial numbers of teenagers, male and female. Political assassins murder men of the caliber of John Kennedy, Martin Luther King Jr., and Robert Kennedy. Today even a few Christian and Jewish American theologians advocate violence as a means of curing social ills.

One who adheres to the Judeo-Christian ethic cannot condone violence. Throughout history this fact has often been

---

[4] 1940 Year Book of Obstetrics and Gynecology 69.

ignored by those who call themselves religious. Even a contemporary theologian such as Werner Schöllgen can argue that the Christian must accept the difference between the Sermon on the Mount and the violent reality of man's world. Such a view reduces the teaching of Christ to a pipedream. Lawyers are not generally considered daydreamers, but they believe that man can overcome his tendency to violence through the rule of law. Should the Christian take any less seriously this teaching of Christ:

> You have learnt how it was said: you must love your neighbor and hate your enemy. But I say to you: love your enemies, and pray for those who persecute you; in this way you will be sons of your father in heaven, for he causes his sun to rise on bad men as well as on the good, and his rain to fall on honest and dishonest men alike. For if you love those who love you, what right have you to claim any credit? Even the tax-collectors do as much, do they not? And if you save your greetings for your brothers, are you doing anything exceptional? Even the pagans do as much, do they not? You must therefore be perfect just as your heavenly Father is perfect (Mt. 5: 43–48).

The Christian has a duty to love even his enemy. He will, of course, recognize that man has a right to defend himself against violence. He will also recognize that law enforcement officers have a moral and legal duty to end civil violence by force. But the Christian rejects violence even against his enemies. He will not attempt to justify the force used by some priests and laymen in Milwaukee to compel a scrub woman to admit them to a government office so that they could protest the violence of Vietnam. He has a moral duty of supporting programs which are aimed at destroying the causes of violence in human society: poverty, overcrowding, prejudice, extreme nationalism, mental illness.

The late Dr. Martin Luther King, Jr. was a Christian theologian. As a leading advocate of non-violence Dr. King had his scholarly roots deep in New Testament studies. He recalled to many Christians of the twentieth century the New Testament advocacy of non-violence. Gandhi was not a Christian. But Gandhi acknowledged that his teaching on social revolution through non-violence was a belief of Jesus. He wrote: "The teaching of the Sermon on the Mount echoed something I had learnt in childhood and something which seemed to be part of my being. . . . This teaching was non-retaliation, or non-resistance to evil." The teaching of Jesus, as echoed by King and Gandhi, has had considerable impact on twentieth-century thought. The deaths of both King and Gandhi indicate that one who lives by non-violence must be prepared to lose his life at the hands of evil, that the triumph of the non-violent will be ultimate rather than immediate. But certainly the life and death of Jesus Christ made that fact clear twenty centuries ago.

Non-violence as a moral means of improving society does not provide a practicable answer to the problem of violence in urban America. Violence is glorified throughout American society. The most disturbing form of pornography, the glorification of violence, is everywhere. "Children's" cartoons on television make violence a central theme. Commercial advertising frequently condones aggressive activity. Children's toys idealize violence. Films portray aggression as normal and expected. School texts contain favorable references to war. Physical violence is presented as a means to orderly social organization on television. Aberrant behavior involving violence is detailed in the press. The most we can hope for is that the growing acceptance of Christian non-violence will diminish this glorification of violence and replace it with idealization of the rule of law.

There are some who are pessimistic about the future of man because of urban violence. While he still has a long way to go in his nonviolent evolution, man has progressed toward the rule of law. But he rightly lives in fear of the violence perpetrated against him by the industrial complex which poisons his air and water. He is properly disturbed by the aggression which results from overcrowding and lack of space in the cities. He should be alarmed by the danger of nuclear or chemical destruction and the diminished but continuing influence of military men in modern society. The Judeo-Christian religion does not insure man that he will not disappear from history, but it does ask him to be optimistic in spite of these fears. Paul Tillich has expressed the reason for this optimism:

> What has the Christian message to say? . . . it tells us nothing about the duration of human history. It does not say that it will continue after tomorrow, nor how it will come to an end in scientific terms. None of this is its concern . . . If history should end tomorrow, through mankind's self-annihilation, the appearance of this planet and of man upon it will not have been in vain . . . At least once, a living being shall have come into existence in whom life achieved its highest possibility—spirit. This is the ultimate source of man's greatness, and those of us who openly or covertly accuse life should open ourselves to this truth: in the short span of our life and the short span of human history and even of the existence of this planet, something of eternal significance did happen—the depth of all things became manifest in one being, and the name of that being is man, and you and I are men.[5]

---

[5] *The Eternal Now*, N.Y.: Charles Scribner's Sons, (1963).

CHAPTER IV

THE LIFE OF THE FAMILY

The Family's Right to Privacy

In any list of fundamental human rights, the right to be let alone should appear in a prominent place. This may be a modern heresy since the growing emphasis on community orientation creates a great distrust of solitude. No area of the common law has developed so slowly and with so many qualifications as the right to privacy. Moralists write with distrust of the man who seeks to absent himself from the community for a time. Yet the human spirit craves solitude. Jesus, the most community-minded of men, sought to be by himself or with small groups of friends on many occasions. So has every great thinker, writer, and leader in human history. It could be said that no man can be truly human unless he can be by himself every so often. The right to privacy which the individual needs to survive in a human condition is also required by the family. No family can hope to grow, create and become meaningful to its members unless those members have time exclusively for each other.

There is reason to be concerned that the family, like the individual, is losing its privacy. Our schools take the children from the home for a great number of hours each week and allow parents little choice as to what elements go into the education of that child. The law sometimes obtrusively forces itself into the family relation where its presence is neither needed or wanted. Obscenity abounds and intrudes into the minds of children when they are outside the family shelter.

Computerized data in the hands of both government and commercial enterprise enable non-family members to learn things about the family which once would have been considered private information. Certainly we must begin to protect the right of the family to exercise certain of its fundamental functions with maximum freedom from interference by outside forces.

The law has long protected the family from certain forms of gross interference. The sanctity of the home, for example, is one of the glories of Anglo-American law. It was summarized by William Pitt in the 18th century:

> The poorest man may in his cottage bid defiance to all the force of the Crown. It may be frail; its roof may shake; the wind may blow through it; the storms may enter, the rain may enter,—but the King of England cannot enter; all his forces dare not cross the threshold of the ruined tenement!

One of the major causes of the American Revolution was the resentment of the people over the forced quartering of British soldiers in their homes. This deprived them of a right to familial privacy which Englishmen had long enjoyed. The Bill of Rights of the United States Constitution provided for "the right of the people to be secure in their . . . homes . . . against unreasonable search and seizure." While the law approves certain forms of electronic "bugging," the privacy of a family in their own homes is and must remain inviolable. Sometime between October 1961, and October 1962, Clifford Eastman allegedly placed a listening device in the bedroom of a home which he rented to Mr. and Mrs. Carl Hamberger in Gilford, New Hampshire. When the Hambergers discovered this, they sued Eastman to recover damages for invasion of privacy. In allowing the suit Chief Justice Kenison of the Superior Court of New Hampshire wrote:

> If the peeping Tom, the big ear and the electronic eavesdropper have a place in the hierarchy of social values, it ought not to be at the expense of a married couple minding their own business in the seclusion of their bedroom who have never asked for or by their conduct deserved a potential pro-

jection of their private conversations and actions to their landlord or to others. Whether actual or potential, such publicity with respect to private matters of purely personal concern is an injury to personality. It impairs the mental peace and comfort of the individual and may produce suffering more acute than that produced by a mere bodily injury. The use of parabolic microphones and sonic wave devices designed to pick up conversations in a room without entering it and at a considerable distance away makes the problem far from fanciful.

For the purposes of the present case it is sufficient to hold that the invasion of the plaintiffs' solitude or seclusion, as alleged in the pleadings, was a violation of their right of privacy and constituted a tort for which the plaintiffs may recover damages; to the extent that they can prove them. Certainly, no right deserves greater protection, for, as Emerson has well said, "solitude, the safeguard of mediocrity, is to genius the stern friend."

The four kinds of invasion comprising the law of privacy include intrusion upon the plaintiff's physical and mental solitude or seclusion. We have not searched for cases where the bedroom of husband and wife has been "bugged" but it should not be necessary—by way of understatement—to observe that this is the type of intrusion that would be offensive to any person of ordinary sensibilities. What married people do in the privacy of their bedroom is their own business so long as they are not hurting anyone else. A person who unreasonably and seriously interferes with another's interest in not having his affairs known to others is liable to the other. It is only where the intrusion has gone beyond the limits of decency that liability accrues. These limits are exceeded where intimate details of the life of one who has never manifested a desire to have publicity are exposed to the public.[1]

The law has always recognized that what a man says to his wife, or vice versa, is a confidential communication like the conversation between a lawyer and a client. A spouse can object to the introduction of such a confidential communication in court. It is also generally recognized that one spouse cannot be compelled to testify against the other in a criminal prosecution. In 1958, the United States Supreme Court even

---

[1] Hamberger v. Eastman 206 A.2d 239 (1965).

reversed the conviction of a man whose wife had voluntarily testified against him. Mr. Justice Black wrote:

> The basic reason the law has refused to pit wife against husband or husband against wife in a trial where life or liberty is at stake was a belief that such a policy was necessary to foster family peace, not only for the benefit of husband, wife and children, but for the benefit of the public as well. Such a belief has never been unreasonable and is not now. Moreover, it is difficult to see how family harmony is less disturbed by a wife's voluntary testimony against her husband than by her compelled testimony. In truth, it seems probable that much more bitterness would be engendered by voluntary testimony than by that which is compelled. But the Government argues that the fact a husband or wife testifies against the other voluntarily is strong indication that the marriage is already gone. Doubtless this is often true. But not all marital flare-ups in which one spouse wants to hurt the other are permanent. The widespread success achieved by courts throughout the country in conciliating family differences is a real indication that some apparently broken homes can be saved provided no unforgivable act is done by either party. Adverse testimony given in criminal proceedings would, we think, be likely to destroy almost any marriage.[2]

Originally, a husband and wife could not even be prosecuted for conspiracy because of the intimate and private relation existing between them. In June, 1960, the Supreme Court decided that the federal government could no longer be prevented from conducting such prosecutions:

> The fact of the matter is that we are asked to write into law a doctrine that parrot-like has been repeated in decisions and texts from what was given its authoritative expression by Hawkins early in the eighteenth century. He wrote: "It plainly appears from the Words of the Statute, That one Person alone cannot be guilty of Conspiracy within the Purport of it; from whence it follows, . . . That no such Prosecution is maintainable against a Husband and Wife only, because they are esteemed but as one Person in Law, and are presumed to have but one Will."
>
> It is revolting to have no better reason for a rule of law

---

[2] U.S. v. Hawkins 358 U.S. 74 (1958).

than that so it was laid down in the time of Henry IV. It is still more revolting if the grounds upon which it was laid down have vanished long since, and the rule simply persists from blind imitation of the past." Holmes, *Collected Legal Papers*, 187 (1920), reprinting *The Path of the Law*, 10 *Harv L Rev* 457, 469 (1897).

For this Court now to act on Hawkins's formulation of the medieval view that husband and wife are esteemed but as one Person in Law, and are presumed to have but one Will would indeed be blind imitation of the past.

But the vigorous dissent of Chief Justice Warren eloquently expressed the belief that marital relation is of greater importance to our society than even efficient law enforcement:

It is not necessary to be wedded to fictions to approve the husband-wife conspiracy doctrine, for one of the dangers which that doctrine averts is the prosecution and conviction of persons for "conspiracies" which Congress never meant to be included within the statute. A wife, simply by virtue of the intimate life she shares with her husband, might easily perform acts that would technically be sufficient to involve her in a criminal conspiracy with him, but which might be far removed from the arm's-length agreement typical of that crime. It is not a medieval mental quirk or an attitude "unnourished by sense" to believe that husbands and wives should not be subjected to such a risk, or that such a possibility should not be committed to endanger the confidentiality of the marriage relationship. While it is easy enough to ridicule Hawkins' pronouncement in Pleas of the Crown from a metaphysical point of view, the concept of the "oneness" of a married couple may reflect an abiding belief that the communion between husband and wife is such that their actions are not always to be regarded by the criminal law as if there were no marriage.

One need not waver in his belief in virile law enforcement to insist that there are other things in American life which are also of great importance, and to which even law enforcement must accommodate itself. One of these is the solidarity and the confidential relationship of marriage.[3]

The United States Supreme Court explicitly recognized a right to family privacy for the first time in 1965. A Connecti-

[3] U.S. v. Dedge 364 U.S. 51 (1960).

cue law made it a crime to use any drug or article for the prevention of conception. Dr. Griswold, Professor of Medicine at the Yale Medical School, prescribed a contraception device for a married couple and was arrested as accessory to the crime. Griswold was convicted and fined. In reversing his conviction the Supreme Court stressed the right of the family to privacy:

(Mr. Justice Douglas)

The present case, then, concerns a relationship lying within the zone of privacy created by several fundamental constitutional guarantees. And it concerns a law which, in forbidding the use of contraceptives rather than regulating their manufacture or sale, seeks to achieve its goals by means having a maximum destructive impact upon that relationship. Such a law cannot stand. Would we allow the police to search the sacred precincts of marital bedrooms for telltale signs of the use of contraceptives? The very idea is repulsive to the notions of privacy surrounding the marriage relationship.

We deal with a right of privacy older than the Bill of Rights—older than our political parties, older than our school system. Marriage is a coming together for better or for worse, hopefully enduring, and intimate to the degree of being sacred. It is an association that promotes a way of life, not causes; a harmony in living, not political faiths; a bilateral loyalty, not commercial or social projects. Yet it is an association for as noble a purpose as any involved in our prior decisions.

(Mr. Justice Goldberg)

The Connecticut statutes here involved deal with a particularly important and sensitive area of privacy—that of the marital relation and the marital home. The right to marry, establish a home and bring up children is an essential part of the liberty guaranteed by the Fourteenth Amendment. In Pierce v. Society of Sisters, the Court held unconstitutional an Oregon Act which forbade parents from sending their children to private schools because such an act unreasonably interferes with the liberty of parents and guardians to direct the upbringing and education of children under their control.

I agree with Mr. Justice Harlan's statement: "Certainly the safeguarding of the home does not follow merely from the sanctity of property rights. The home derives its preeminence as the seat of family life. And the integrity of that life is something so fundamental that it has been found to draw to its protection the principles of more than one explicitly granted Constitutional right. . . . Of this whole 'private realm of family life' it is difficult to imagine what is more private or more intimate than a husband and wife's marital relations."

The entire fabric of the Constitution and the purposes that clearly underlie its specific guarantees demonstrate that the rights to marital privacy and to marry and raise a family are of similar order and magnitude as the fundamental rights specifically protected.

Although the Constitution does not speak in so many words of the right of privacy in marriage, I cannot believe that it offers these fundamental rights no protection. The fact that no particular provision of the Constitution explicitly forbids the State from disrupting the traditional relation of the family—a relation as old and as fundamental as our entire civilization—surely does not show that the Government was meant to have the power to do so. Rather, as the Ninth Amendment expressly recognizes, there are fundamental personal rights such as this one, which are protected from abridgment by the Government though not specifically mentioned in the Constitution. . . .[4]

When a family moves into a new neighborhood, they are frequently greeted by a "Welcome Wagon." In the glow of happy excitement they accept small tokens of greeting from their new neighbors and answer questions about themselves. What they do not know is that the information they have revealed about their financial status, religion, employment and marriage may be sold to local merchants and credit agencies. This is only one example of a growing trend toward data collection and processing which threatens to strip the American family of much of its traditional privacy. Private credit bureaus, government agencies such as the F.B.I., Civil Service, Defense Department, Internal Revenue, Federal Housing Administration, and industrial investigation agencies maintain vast files which could provide a quite personal view of many American families.

---

[4] Griswold v. Connecticut 381 U.S. 479 (1965).

To survive in our world, the American family must reveal the information which is the basis for the data to governmental and private agencies. Data on the "marital stability" of mortgage seekers which has been provided to the Federal Housing Administration supposedly in confidence can be purchased by banks for $1.50. A party with the money can purchase information on the intimate personal and financial lives of most American families from diverse sources. Book clubs, state agencies and even religious orders will sell lists of their clients or contributors. Psychological research has even probed the mind of many citizens at one time or another, and there is no effective legal safeguard against misuse of the data collected thereby. Alan Weston, in *Privacy and Freedom* (Anthenaeum, 1967) has written of these and other invasions into our private lives which should frighten and alarm every man. Basically it is a moral problem: how far may one intrude into the privacy of a family before his collection of data on that family violates human decency? May commercial desirability, or even governmental need, justify the collection of data which destroys the right of the family to privacy? But, while it is a moral problem, the fact of data collection today requires the closer regulation of the law. When the moral conscience of business and government is not sufficiently formed on this question the law must provide protection to the family.

In some respects the Code of Canon Law of the Roman Catholic Church does sometimes intrude into the privacy of family life in a way which violates the fundamental rights of the members of the family. Certainly the church, like the state, can legislate to promote the good of family life for its members. The Bishops of the Second Vatican Council taught that parents have an "inalienable duty and right" to educate children. That the parent is the primary educator has been a principle of the Christian theology of marital life for centuries. But does Canon Law recognize this right in both fact and practice? Canon 1215 requires that Catholic children be taught in schools where "religious and moral training occupy first place." Canon 1374 forbids parents to send their children to "non-Catholic, indifferent schools that are mixed." The language of these canons may appear quaint to American Catholics, but it is a blatant example of the law's failure to recognize basic parental rights. In many a diocese, and many an American parish, immoral pressures are brought to bear on parents to send their children to church-sponsored schools. It has not been unknown for pastors to tell their parishioners that the child "must attend the Catholic school under pain of mortal sin." Far worse are the discriminations which sometimes exist in the parish against children who do not attend the Catholic school. Some small examples illustrate this. It is not uncommon for Catholic children attending public school to be excluded from the altar boy's society, the choir, or parish festivals. Parents are sometimes made to feel unwelcome in a parish because they have exercised their fundamental right to educate their child as they believe best. The law of the church is at fault as long as it fails to forbid such discrimination.

In 1951, Henry A. Gau was excommunicated by the bishop of St. Cloud, Minnesota, for his public support of a bond issue to build a public high school. Canon Law must forbid such arbitrary exercises of ecclesiastical power. The law must encourage the leaders of the church to develop their power over men from a base of service, not compulsion.

There are other examples of unwarranted intrusion of church law into the privacy of the family. For example, the requirement of a church ritual as a condition for the *validity* of marriage, or the canons creating impediments such as ordination which restrict the right to marry validly. The promise of reform of the law relating to marriage made by Pope Paul VI raises hope that a positive Canon Law will evolve in the future. Pope Paul, by his decree *Matrimonii Sacramentum*, has removed a most immoral intrusion into familial privacy from Catholic practice. By terminating the written promise required of a non-Catholic spouse that he would raise the children as Catholics, the Pope clearly rec-

ognized the right and duty of both parents to raise and educate their children according to their consciences.

Parents, Education, and Public Funds

Ever since the "public" school system began to evolve in
the United States in the middle of the nineteenth century,
there has been great public tension over the status of "private"
schools, especially church-related schools. The courts have
upheld the right of parents to send their children to church-
affiliated accredited schools. But how far may the state go in
allowing parents to exercise this freedom of choice? Must the
state allow maximum freedom of choice in schools by use of
tax monies to aid in the support of educational institutions
which are alternatives to the public school system? Is the state
under a duty to provide certain forms of help and protection
to students who choose to attend non-public schools? How
"private" is a church-related school which meets the accredi-
tation standards of the state and reduces the tax rate by educating substantial numbers of students outside of the public
school structure? To what extent, if any, may private and
public schools cooperate in work of education through expenditure of public monies? May aid be given to church-
related schools without breaching the wall of separation
between church and state which is erected by the First
Amendment of the United States Constitution if the absence
of such aid means the end of church schools? These questions
are not new. Almost a century ago President Grant expressed
support for the classical separatist doctrine which has remained
the basic issue in these questions:

> Encourage free schools, and resolve that not one dollar
> appropriated for their support shall be appropriated to the
> court of any sectarian schools. Resolve that neither the state
> nor nation, nor both combined, shall support institutions of
> learning other than those sufficient to afford every child grow-
> ing up in the land the opportunity of a good common-school
> education unmixed with sectarian, pagan, or atheistical dog-
> mas. Leave the matter of religion to the family altar, the

church, and the private school, supported entirely by private contributions. Keep the church and the state forever separate.[5]

To what extent is this doctrine desirable today?

In 1966 the Horace Mann League sought an injunction against several church-related colleges and certain officials of the state of Maryland to prevent the colleges from receiving $2,500,000 in state aid. The state aid consisted of matching funds for the construction of dining halls and science buildings. The Court of Appeals of the state of Maryland ruled that the aid violated both the Maryland and United States Constitutions. Two of the schools, Western Maryland College and Notre Dame College, sought the grants to construct science buildings. Western Maryland College received about 2% to 3% of its operating capital from the Methodist Church and required programs of religious services for its students; ⅓ of its governing board must be Methodist clergymen, 40% of its student body is Methodist. It conducts a pre-ministerial study program, and publishes college literature characterizing the school as a "religiously oriented institution." Notre Dame College advertises itself as having a "Catholic atmosphere," has many nuns on the faculty who are appointed to the college by the sister-superior of the order (in "consultation" with the college president who is a "subject" of that superior), and has a student body which is 97% Catholic. Each class (including those which would be held in the new science building) begins with a prayer, and the college states in its publications that its entire college program harmonizes "with the philosophy and theology of the Catholic Church." In denying state aid Chief Judge Prescott wrote:

> The problem to be considered and solved when the First Amendment was proposed was not one of hazy or comparative insignificance, but was one of blunt and stark reality, which had perplexed and plagued the nations of Western Civilization for some 14 centuries, and during that long period, the union

---

[5] "The President's Speech at Des Moines," *Catholic World* Vol. 22, p. 434, (1876).

of Church and State in the government of man had produced neither peace on earth, nor good will to man.

In an attempt to prevent recurrences of many of the unfortunate evils mentioned above . . . our forebears decided it was best for Government, best for Religion and best for mankind that the two be kept separate and apart. In order to effectuate this goal, the First Amendment was adopted which provides that "Congress shall make no law respecting an establishment of religion, or prohibiting the free exercise thereof."

We shall not repeat all of what we said above concerning the College's activities. We find nothing on the face of the bill or its legislative history to demonstrate a purpose to use the State's coercive power to aid religion, but a careful consideration of all the facts impels us to the conclusion that the operative effect will be such, if the grant be effectuated. The most effective way to establish any institution is to finance it. . . . Financing a church either in its strictly religious activities or in its other activities is equally unconstitutional: how can it seriously be argued that a grant of tax-raised funds to such an institution would not be "to support . . . religious activities or institutions, whatever they may be called or whatever form they may adopt to teach or practice religion"?

The operative effect of the Bills (if the grants are permitted to be made) demonstrates, in a legal constitutional sense, a purpose to use the State's coercive power to aid religion; that grants, if made, would constitute a contribution by the State of tax-raised funds to support institutions which teach the tenets and faith of a particular church; and that the taxes levied to raise the funds for the grants would be levied to help support religious activities and religious institutions.

We agree with Neil J. McCluskey, S.J., in his work *Catholic Viewpoint on Education*, p. 168, wherein he stated: "The Catholic laity and clergy are fully aware that direct basic support by the government to parochial schools is out of the question" because the U.S. Supreme Court would interpret such action as a contravention of the Federal Constitution.

Judge Hammond dissented from this conclusion:

I think that the four grants under consideration were made pursuant to long-established practice to further a secular public purpose and that any aid or benefit flowing from them to religion would be slight, vague and purely incidental. The grants will supply added facilities which will help the secular educational activities of religious groups and will aid students who now and hereafter attend the institutions and the people of the State of Maryland by increasing the number of those who can receive a college education and the quality of the education that the increased number will receive. The grants will not aid religion or a religious group; those who attend college are or are not at that age religiously inclined and if they are, have, in almost all cases, become attached to a particular faith. Students are not proselytized at any of the four donee colleges. It will not aid religion or the Catholic Church for more students, mostly Catholic, to be able to attend St. Joseph or Notre Dame, or the Methodist Church for more students, largely Methodists, to attend Western Maryland College (and in both cases to receive perhaps a better education because of the grants) to a degree greater than it will society in general.

There is no reasonable alternative to State aid to private institutions of higher learning. Theoretically, the State might enlarge State colleges enough to care for all actual and potential students or create new public colleges to do so. Tremendous sums would be required in either case and, what is more important, available physical facilities and faculty and administrative staffs could not be produced for years. In the Note, *Constitutionality of Federal Financial Aid to Church-Related Colleges* (77 Harv. L. Rev. 1353, p. 1358), the author points out that of the 2,000 institutions of higher learning in the United States 800 are church-related, and says:

> To exclude these 800 institutions of higher learning from federal aid would seriously hamper the effort to increase enrollment capacity to the point where colleges will be able to handle the expected demand of 1970 and distort the present educational allocation of students between denominational and nondenominational schools . . . Such pragmatic considerations would be irrelevant if the command of the Constitution were clear; the remedy would then be a constitutional amendment. However, the lack of an effective alternative should be highly relevant when a plausible constitutional defense can be made and where, in an area of church-state overlap, criteria can be formulated which minimize governmental intrusion into religious concerns without paralyzing governmental attempts to cope with urgent national problems.[6]

---

[6] Horace Mann League v. Maryland, 220 A.2d 51 (1966).

On February 27, 1963, the legislature of Rhode Island adopted a statute which required local school committees (i.e., school boards) to lend mathematics, science and language textbooks to all elementary and secondary school students living in the community. Early in 1968, a group of taxpayers sought a court order against such loans to students of non-public schools. Judge Perkins issued the restraining order, basing his decision on the separation of church and state:

> The religious aspects of the schools involved attended by pupils to whom the textbooks are loaned must of course receive consideration. As to the Providence Hebrew Day School, it has been stipulated that it is operated, among other purposes, for instructing and teaching the Jewish religion in elementary grades. As to St. Paul's Evangelical Lutheran Church, no evidence was presented. As regards the parochial schools, the operation and conduct of which are supervised by the Roman Catholic Diocese, the evidence before the Court is contained in an exhibit consisting of a handbook of school regulations of the Diocese of Providence including such schools. Since at times in the course of argument there seems to have been faint denial of the fact that these were church schools strongly dedicated to the teaching of religion it seems pertinent to call attention to certain of the statements in that handbook. At page 2 there is quoted from the Fourth Diocesan Synod, Stat. 351.1, the following:

> > The Diocesan School Board, with the Bishop presiding, shall supervise the education, both spiritual and secular, in the parochial schools, and diocesan high shools.

> At page 4 there is also quoted from Stat. 353.1 the following:

> > The pastor shall have full charge of the parochial school under the direction of the Diocesan Board of Education and the Diocesan Superintendent of Schools.

> At page 14 these elementary schools are referred to as "Catholic schools"; at page 15 the Mass is stipulated to be celebrated at the beginning of each school year. At page 16 it is provided that systematic religious instructions must be provided in all schools. At page 21 reference is again made to each school as a "Catholic school." At page 28 covering regulations in regard to the textbook law itself the schools are

once more referred to as "Catholic." At page 39 a schedule of reasonably sufficient daily prayers is set forth, including those to be taken at the opening of the school day, after recess, at noon dismissal, at the beginning of the afternoon sessions, and at dismissal. At page 55 it designates Religion, English and Mathematics as "major subjects, all others minor." At page 58 "the end of Catholic education" is set forth as "the formation of Christ in those regenerated by Baptism." At page 63 there appears a sample contract for all lay teachers made directly with the pastor of the Church who is the head of the school involved. And of course it is common knowledge and appears within the handbook that nuns and priests teach in addition to the lay teachers. At page 50 it appears that "The Diocese of Providence supports the ideal of a Catholic secondary education for every Catholic who desires it," an assertion, it is true, related to secondary schools, but with no reason to believe that the statement is not applicable to elementary schools.

In the case of furnishing of textbooks the expenditure of public moneys does not stop at the door to the school but overflows into the school itself and takes care of part of the education there taking place. Public funds are there expended for the essential functioning of the school itself, a school under religious auspices the support of which basically is banned by the First Amendment.

The Court is persuaded that the line must in any case be drawn at the entrance to the school. It is there that the educational process begins. It may be mixing the concrete with the theoretical but the outer wall of religious school must clearly be the inner wall of separation of church and state if the existence of that wall is to continue in any meaningful manner.[7]

The problem facing the court in these cases differed from situation which was presented to the United States Supreme Court in an earlier case. Everson, a New Jersey taxpayer, challenged the right of a local school board to reimburse parents for the cost of transporting their children to non-public schools. Writing for the majority of the Court, Mr. Justice Black upheld the right of New Jersey to provide money for the transportation of children to religious schools:

---

[7] Bowerman v. O'Connor, Equity No. 31775 (R.I. Superior Court).

The "establishment of religion" clause of the First Amendment means at least this: Neither a state nor the Federal Government can set up a church. Neither can pass laws which aid one religion, aid all religions, or prefer one religion over another. Neither can force nor influence a person to go to or to remain away from church against his will or force him to profess a belief or disbelief in any religion. No person can be punished for entertaining or professing religious beliefs or disbeliefs, for church attendance or non-attendance. No tax in any amount, large or small, can be levied to support any religious activities or institutions, whatever they may be called, or whatever form they may adopt to teach or practice religion. Neither a state nor the Federal Government can, openly or secretly, participate in the affairs of any religious organizations or groups and vice versa. In the words of Jefferson, the clause against establishment of religion by law was intended to erect "a wall of separation between church and State." The amendment commands that New Jersey cannot hamper its citizens in the free exercise of their own religion. Consequently, it cannot exclude individual Catholics, Lutherans, Mohammedans, Baptists, Jews, Methodists, Non-believers, Presbyterians, or the members of any other faith, because of their faith, or lack of it, from receiving the benefits of public welfare legislation. While we do not mean to intimate that a state could not provide transportation only for children attending public schools, we must be careful, in protecting the citizens of New Jersey against state-established churches, to be sure that we do not inadvertently prohibit New Jersey from extending its general state law to all its citizens without regard to their religious belief.

Measured by these standards, we cannot say that the First Amendment prohibits New Jersey from spending tax-raised funds to pay the bus fares of parochial school pupils as a part of a general program under which it pays the fares of pupils attending public and other schools.

This Court has said that parents may, in the discharge of their duty under state compulsory education laws, send their children to a religious rather than a public school if the school meets the secular educational requirements which the state has the power to impose. See Pierce v. Society of Sisters, 268 U.S. 510. It appears that these parochial schools meet New Jersey's requirements. The State contributes no money to the schools. It does not support them. Its legislation, as applied, does no more than provide a general program to help parents

get their children, regardless of their religion, safely and ex-
peditiously to and from accredited schools.

The First Amendment has erected a wall between church
and state. That wall must be kept high and impregnable. We
could not approve the slightest breach. New Jersey has not
breached it here.[8]

The Everson case is distinguished from the Maryland and
Rhode Island decisions by the fact that no direct aid from
public money was made to the religious *schools* by New
Jersey. It would be a fair statement of the present status of the
law to say that the First Amendment forbids any direct governmental aid to schools which in any way assists or promotes
religion. Thus a Virginia court invalidated state tuition for
orphans of soldiers if the tuition was to be paid to religious
schools (1955), a Vermont court forbade payment of tuition
for parochial school students (1961), and a Kentucky court
struck down a tax exemption for parents who sent their children to parochial schools (1892). Whether a state grant giving
free textbooks to children attending religious schools constitutes an unlawful establishment of religion, as the Rhode
Island court decided, is much disputed. In 1967, a New York
court ruled that such aid was lawful, as did a Louisiana court
in 1929, and a Mississippi court in 1941. The United States
Supreme Court recently affirmed the result in the New York
case. But an Oregon court in 1961 took the position that free
textbooks for students of religious schools would be direct aid
to religion. However, direct tax exemptions for religious
schools (excusing them from paying property taxes, for ex·
ample) have been upheld by the courts.

In view of the fact that church-related schools already constitute a substantial part of the American educational structure, a number of people today ask whether direct aid to religious schools for non-religious purposes is not a pragmatic
necessity. There is growing evidence that such schools cannot
continue to meet contemporary educational demands without

---

[8] Everson v. Board of Education 330 U.S. 1 (1947).

state aid. Yet any serious decline in church-sponsored educational institutions would cause havoc in a public school system whose tax base is already close to a maximum point. Our interpretation of the Constitution cannot be based on economic necessity, but it must be asked if the desperate need of our nation should not cause us to re-think the question of what constitutes direct aid to religion. Certainly the Citizens for Educational Freedom have stated a strong case for aid to parents as the basis of freedom of choice in education. From the neighborhood school, to direct election of school boards, to P.T.A.s, the United States has a long history of relating the home and school. From both a moral and a cultural viewpoint it would seem desirable for parents to have a true choice of schools available to them. Such a choice can be available only to the very wealthy unless a healthy extensive system of private education is available in the United States. The exclusion of all forms of religious indoctrination and prayer from the public school made this quite apparent.

There are many Christians who question whether parents really have a choice in education at all today. I have publicly questioned whether Catholic schools really provide the alternative of religious education when the religion teachers are so frequently untrained and incompetent. Some people reject state aid on the grounds that government assistance would ultimately move the schools closer to religious neutrality, thus diminishing still further parental choice. Others have asked if programs such as shared time or released time, with parents and churches free to develop their own programs, might not constitute a better alternative to religious schools. Whatever the answer, the United States cannot any longer fail to come to grips with the twofold problem of declining quality in private schools and declining freedom on the part of parents. If the expenditure of public monies is the only way in which the right of the parent to educate his children freely can be maintained we will have to consider this one of the prices we pay to maintain a free society.

Adoption, the Law, and the Christian

Betty Jean Tuttle was born in Pittsburgh, Pennsylvania, in January, 1944. Her mother was not married, and immediately turned Betty Jean over to a foundling asylum. When she became too old for the asylum, in May, 1945, Betty was turned over to the Children's Aid Society. The Society was made Betty Jean's legal guardian. In May, 1945, a Mr. and Mrs. Gard applied to the society to adopt a child. The Society discouraged the Gards from adopting a child, but informed the couple that they had a little girl for whom they could provide a foster home. Betty Jean went home with the Gards in June, 1945. In December, 1945, Mr. and Mrs. Gard asked if they could adopt Betty Jean; in June, 1946, Betty Jean's natural mother signed a release allowing the Society to arrange for an adoption. The Society then demanded that Betty Jean be returned to it. The Gards refused to return Betty Jean. In July, 1947, the Society filed a writ of habeus corpus asking that the court order the Gards to return Betty Jean. The court refused to issue the order. In 1949, the Supreme Court of Pennsylvania affirmed the action of the trial court. Wrote Chief Justice Maxey:

> A child of two years of age or under will form new attach-
> ments quickly if treated kindly by those into whose care it is
> given. In that respect it resembles a young tree whose roots
> have not yet taken deep hold in the nourishing earth, but
> when a child is much beyond the age of two years, it becomes
> strongly attached to those who stand in parental relationship
> to it and who have tenderly cared for it. Its bonds of affection
> have become so strong that to sunder them suddenly may
> result not only in the child's unhappiness, but also in its
> physical injury. Even dogs which have been separated from
> masters to whom they are attached have been known to go
> into physical decline and sometimes to die as a result of that
> separation. To take this nearly 65 months old girl, Betty Jean
> Tuttle, away from the only parents she has known since she
> was an infant of eighteen months would be exactly the same

in its effect on her and on the man and woman who have stood in a parental relationship to her for nearly four years as would the separation of any well cared for child from its own parents. Nothing could be more cruel than the forceable separation of a child from either its real or foster parents by whom it is bound by strong ties of affection; to a child it is equally cruel whether the separation is brought about by "kidnapping" or by legal process. In passing on the contested custody of children no judge can do justice without considering the human aspect of his problem.

The contention made in this case, that it would be better for the child to be taken from its present home and given into the hands of persons it does not know and whose identity has never been revealed, because of the so-called "illegitimacy" of this child's birth, is an argument of such little weight as to require no refutation. It is well known that Nature in endowing children at their creation with gifts of spirit, mind and body never discriminates against the so-called "illegitimate," and the circumstance of their birth has been no blight upon their careers. Some of the greatest men and women in history were born out of wedlock. A man who served as Prime Minister of Great Britain during the present century and another exceptionally able man, who had a very large part in the establishment of the Federal Union in the last two decades of the 18th century, were so-called "illegitimate" children, but that "bar sinister" did not bar their advancement and, apparently, caused them no personal disquietude. Now to separate this little girl from Mr. and Mrs. Gard would cause her far more anguish than any possible future malicious taunt as to the circumstances of her birth.

Societies which are entrusted by the sovereign with power over the lives of infants should ever bear in mind that consideration for the sensibilities of children and solicitude for their well-being is the hallmark of an humane individual and of a civilized state.[9]

Why was not Betty Jean put up for adoption shortly after her birth? Was it because no one asked her mother to release her for adoption? Was the child considered unadoptable? Could it just be that no one cared about Betty Jean? Why were the Gards discouraged from adopting Betty Jean by the

---

[9] Children's Aid Society v. Gard 66 A.2d 300, (1949).

agency? Were they too old? Were they of a different race? Were they of a different religion than Betty Jean's mother? Was it because they had no formal religious beliefs? Were there other persons who had priority over the Gards? If so, why was Betty Jean not made available to them immediately rather than being placed in a foster home? When it became apparent that the Gards were successfully raising Betty Jean why did the officials of the agency oppose the adoption petition? Was the opposition to the adoption based on a sincere belief that the best interests of the child were at stake or on pre-determined agency rules? These are but a few of the problems of current adoption practices. Too often the courts fail, the agencies fail, the churches fail—and children go homeless or drift from foster home to foster home. At root, it is a moral failure of our society. How deep a failure can be grasped from the realization that in most states the court would have taken Betty Jean from the Gards and returned her to the agency.

The distinguished church historian Arthur Mirgeler has pointed out in *Mutations of Western Christianity* that the importance and value of adoption has been minimized in the teaching of the Western Church. He contrasts this with the practice of pre-Christian Rome in which adoption played a constructive and dynamic function in society. This indifference toward adoption is especially difficult to understand since the New Testament speaks of adoption as a most God-like activity. From the moment that St. Paul recognized Jesus as the Christ and realized that through his Church Jesus effects a new relationship between God and man, the Apostle struggled to discover and express the nature of that relationship. Of the many analogies he used few have been so penetrating and influential as that of the adopted son:

> Before we came of age we were as good as slaves to the elemental principles of this world, but when the appointed time came, God sent his Son, born of a woman, born a subject of the Law, to redeem the subjects of the Law and to enable us to be adopted as sons. The proof that you are sons

is that God has sent the Spirit of His Sons into our hearts:
the Spirit that cries, "Abba, Father," and it is this that makes
you a son, you are not a slave any more; and if God has
made you a son, then he has made you heir (Gal 4: 3–7).

In spite of the New Testament use of adoption as an
analogue of the Fatherhood of God, the institutional church
has not shown much interest in encouraging the practice.
The Bishops of Vatican II listed "the adoption of abandoned
infants" first among the recommended "activities of the
family apostolate" (*Decree on the Laity*, §11). But the docu-
ments of the Catholic Church, even those dealing with family
life, rarely refer to adoption. Except for Francis Filas, no contemporary theologian has attempted to deal with adoption in
a moral framework. Many individual Christians do not favor
making adoption a more common practice because of racial
prejudices or irrational fears of illegitimate children.

Church agencies have shown a lack of willingness to fight
the public prejudices which have prevented adoption from
becoming a more positive force in society. The church has
made no concentrated effort to educate the public moral
conscience on this question. Indeed, some church agencies
have sometimes appeared to be more interested in institution-
alizing needy children than in aggressive support of adoption.
In the United States there are right now hundreds of thousands of children who need a home; there are also hundreds of
thousands of capable people who want to adopt children.
That we cannot overcome our prejudices and our lethargy
sufficiently to bring them together manifests a moral failure.

The failure of the church has been complemented by the
apathy of the citizen toward legal reform in the area of adoption. Every major system of law in history recognized the practice of adoption except the English common law from which
American law was derived. With its great emphasis on bloodline heirship English law did not recognize the right of a
family to adopt a child until 1926. Some American states recognized adoption in the mid-nineteenth century, and civil
(Roman) law states such as Texas and Louisiana accepted the
practice. But it was not until the twentieth century that

adoption came into practice on any substantial scale in the
United States. Our historical inexperience with adoption may
account for some of our failures, but we can no longer excuse
ourselves from determining to make adoption a socially bene-
ficial procedure.

A major obstacle to the development of adoption has been
the requirement that the legal custodian or guardian of the
child give his consent to the adoption. This requirment is a
worthwhile attempt to protect the natural parents from the
unjustified loss of their child. But in practice it not infre-
quently results in an intolerable situation for the child. Without abandoning the child in the legal sense, the person whose
consent is required allows the child's tender years to be passed
in an institution or series of foster homes. Pearl Buck has
described the absurdity and immorality of such a situation:

> I visited orphanages to ask why the children were not set
> free for adoption. I was told that the children were not re-
> leased by their legal guardians. This is true. They cannot be
> placed in their loving adoptive families because someone will
> not let them go. But who is that somebody . . . It may be a
> relative, or a judge or a social agency. It may be just the hold
> of a church.
>
> Such parents cry out "I'll never give up my child." And yet
> they do give up their children daily, yearly and for life by keep-
> ing them orphaned. A post card once or twice a year or a taw-
> dry gift at Christmas, suffices to keep children within the letter
> of the law against abandonment. . . .
>
> There is no truth in the much repeated slogan of adoptive
> agencies that there are not enough children for adoption.
> There is a surplus of children, but the parents who are waiting
> are prevented from adopting them . . . by social workers who
> try to have mothers keep illegitimate children, by parents who
> place children in orphanages, yet refuse to release children for
> adoption, by churches that refuse to permit cross religious
> adoptions or insist on operating orphanages.[10]

Another obstacle to the full-flowering of adoption is the
qualifications sometimes demanded of adoptive parents. In
1958, for example, the Supreme Court of Wisconsin revoked

---

[10] Buck, "The Children Waiting," *Woman's Home Companion*, Sept.
1955, p. 33.

a decree of adoption because the adoptive parents were too old; one spouse was fifty, the other was forty-two. In 1955, the Supreme Judicial Court of Massachusetts allowed a Catholic mother to withdraw her consent to adoption when she learned that the adoptive parents were Jewish. In the same year the same court refused an adoption of twin illegitimate children by Jewish parents because the mother of the children was Catholic. The court refused the adoption even though the mother consented both to the adoption and to the children's being raised in the Jewish religion. In 1957, the Maryland Court of Appeals refused an adoption by a Lutheran couple of a child whose mother was Catholic. The court said the couple was also too old: fifty-four and forty-eight.

Each year thousands of children are kept away from loving homes because the potential parents are of a different race, can not provide a private room for the child, work in certain professions, are not "religious," have a different complexion than the child or for any one of many other arbitrary reasons. Some of these requirements are embodied in the laws of the states, some are imposed by administrative agencies or courts, some are rules of the private or public agencies which handle a substantial number of adoptions in America. The fact that most placement adoptions no longer involve agencies indicates the dissatisfaction with these institutions. Private placement, frequently through the mediation of an attorney who special-izes in this work, is becoming more common. Agencies de-nounce the practice as a "gray market," but if the supervising court is humanely alert to the welfare of both the child and adoptive parents, the practice can be quite effective. In any case the laws and practices which regulate adoption in America are in need of serious reorganization by men of intelli-gence and moral sensitivity.

Legal Reform and Family Disorganization

In 1955, the Court of Appeals of the state of Maryland re-versed a decree of divorce. The divorce had been awarded to the husband, Mr. Courson, on grounds of Mrs. Courson's adultery. The reason for the court's reversal of the decree was simple: since Mr. Courson had deserted Mrs. Courson, he was not entitled to a divorce. In the United States divorce is based on a guilt-innocence premise. The courts will give a divorce to the innocent party; if both parties are guilty of a marital wrong then no divorce will be granted. A few states will award a divorce to the "less" guilty party, but generally an "unworthy" wife will not be granted a divorce from an "unworthy" husband. This is but one example of the greatest failing of American family law; litigation is not designed to serve the social needs of the family and society but is built on an "adversary" premise. In no area is American law as deficient as in its attempts to deal with family disorganization.

The Christian believes that the family is the cornerstone of civilization. "The well being of the individual person and of human and Christian Society is intimately linked with the healthy condition of that community produced by marriage and family" (*The Church Today*, §47). Too, the difficulties and problems of married life pose the challenge of marital permanence, the opportunity for husband and wife to grow in love and service to society. But the Christian's views on indissolubility do not excuse him from being concerned with the fact of family disorganization. Indeed, the Canon Law of the Church provides judicial remedies which attempt to deal with the disorganized Christian family, although these provisions are frequently criticized as grossly inadequate. There is a desperate need for reform of the divorce laws of all fifty states. It is sad to observe that even though they profess great concern for family life, Catholics exhibit little interest in seriously reforming the divorce laws of the society in which they live.

The most obvious problem with the law governing divorce is that it is only slightly related to the true problems of family disorganization. Divorce is considered relief for an innocent spouse whose partner is guilty of adultery, cruelty, or desertion. Determination of this guilt is totally unrelated to the effects a divorce will have on children, the emotional needs and problems of the couple, or even the best interests of society. Divorce then becomes a matter of establishing a fact of marital wrong, much as one proves the existence of a trust or the commission of a crime in other judicial proceedings. That the evidence which proves the marital wrong is frequently manufactured for the purposes of the trial only compounds the absurdity of the system.

Another problem with current legal techniques for dealing with family disorganization is the absence of any meaningful counseling for the disorganized family. The family, an institution which involves the deepest interpersonal relationship, is cast into the harsh realities of the judicial adversary proceeding. Even though most divorces are uncontested, the whole structure of the proceeding is based on a premise that an innocent party is attempting to secure justice from a guilty party. That a family is before the court, a family which needs help, is hardly recognized. A few sensitive courts, however, have recognized it. The Divorce Division of the Circuit Court of Cook County in Illinois is one example. Each year almost 20,000 divorce cases are filed in that court. About forty-thousand children will be affected by these suits; thus eighty-thousand human beings will have their lives greatly affected by the decision of the court each year in this one county. In 1964, the judges of the court established a Conciliation Counseling Service in which personal marital counseling is available to at least a limited number of litigants. To those who are able to take advantage of it, the Service provides a voluntary non-advisory procedure for dealing with the disorganized family. This is a modest step. But it is a recognition that something more than the application of legal categories is needed to deal in a humane way with the disorganized family.

In what direction should reform of divorce laws move? The Christian should certainly insist that any relationship as personal as marriage should be dealt with on a personal basis. This would mean an end to the adversary structure of the family court. The court must be re-organized in such a way that it can deal with the family and its members rather than with two contesting litigants. The disorganized family should be dealt with by a judicial body, for as the United States Supreme Court long ago made clear a marriage is not a private contract:

> Marriage is often termed by text writers and in decisions of courts a civil contract—it is something more than a mere contract. The consent of the parties is, of course, essential to its existence, but when the contract to marry is executed by the marriage, a relation between the parties is created which they cannot change. The relation once formed, the law steps in and holds the parties to various obligations and liabilities. It is an institution, in the maintenance of which in its purity the public is deeply interested, for it is the foundation of the family and of society, without which there would be neither civilization nor progress.
>
> When the contracting parties have entered into the married state, they have not so much entered into a contract as into a new relation, the rights, duties, and obligations of which rest not upon their agreement, but upon the general law of the State, statutory or common, which defines and prescribes those rights, duties, and obligations. They are of law, not of contract. It was of contract that the relation should be established, but being established, the power of the parties as to its extent or duration is at an end. Their rights under it are determined by the will of the sovereign, as evidenced by law.[11]

But the judicial body which deals with the disorganized family should be a radically new type of court. It not only should be staffed with excellent psychological and social investigation staffs, but should approach the disorganized family as a group of people who need help. Strict rules of evidence should not apply to the proceedings. The "grounds" for divorce should be abolished. Whatever disposition the court makes in the end should be based not on legal categories but upon the prudential judgment of the judge as to what is best for the family, the spouses and children, and society generally. All aspects of this judgment, separation, divorce, alimony, child custody *etc.* should be determined by the court only after

[11] Maynard v. Hill 125 U.S. 190 (1888).

thoughtful consultation with the investigative and counseling staff. Such a proceeding would obviously require a much greater financial and manpower investment in our family courts than we now make. But if we believe the family is as important as we say it is, it will be worth the investment.

In a society in which divorce is commonly accepted, the attitude of the Christian church toward its divorced members who have remarried is of great importance. While theologians and canon lawyers have recently been exploring the whole question of the dissolubility of marriage, ecclesiastical conduct toward the divorced member can be either an example of Christian love and understanding or of formalistic scorn. That the attitude of the church has often been the latter is apparent. J. Emerson has shown the un-Christian attitude of the Protestant denominations in *Divorce, the Church and Remarriage.* A Catholic canon lawyer, James Hertel, has contrasted current Catholic attitudes to the Christ-like attitude which might be brought to the human problems of some re-married divorcees:

> There are countless couples today who are "living in sin" simply because they have exercised their freedom as adopted sons of God to marry again in the face of a doubtful first union. Far from living in sin, very many of these couples manifest Christ's loving union with His Church in a marked degree —to such a degree, in fact, that a thoughtful Christian finds it hard to believe the Law of Christ is being violated. The laws of the Church must be framed in such a way that the Christian will realize that, in freely observing them, he is bearing true witness to the Word of God and thereby serving his fellow Christians. Resting firmly upon Scripture and theology, they must be an authentic expression of that freedom wherewith Christ has made us free.[12]

---

[12] Hertel, "Save The Bond or Save The Person?" *America,* Feb. 17, 1968, p. 220.

CHAPTER V

THE LIFE OF THE CIVIL COMMUNITY

The Question of a "Just War"

The God of Israel promised that in the day of the Messiah "I will break bow, sword and battle in the country, and make her sleep secure" (Hosea 2:18). Yet man does not know peace, even in the form of the absence of aggressive war. Throughout the history of the Christian church there have been those who insisted that the Messianic age can be advanced only when the believer refuses to do violence even to the violent. When the armed representatives of the chief priests illegally seized Jesus, Peter drew his sword in defense of the Master:

> Then they came forward, seized Jesus and took him in charge. At that, one of the followers of Jesus grasped his sword and drew it; he struck out at the high priest's servant, and cut off his ear. Jesus then said, "Put your sword back, for all who draw the sword will die by the sword." (Matt 26:50–52).

From the age of the Apostles to the twentieth century there have been those, such as the gentle Francis of Assisi, who taught that Christianity and violence are incompatible. Yet most Christian moralists have not subscribed to that belief; they have taught that both the individual and the community can morally defend themselves against unjustified aggression. The Bishops of the Second Vatican Council, while praising those who reject violence as a defense, did not condemn those who teach self-defense:

All Christians are urgently summoned "to practice the truth in love" (Eph. 4:15) and to join with all true peacemakers in pleading for peace and bringing it about.

Motivated by this same spirit, we cannot fail to praise those who renounce the use of violence in the vindication of their rights and who resort to methods of defense which are otherwise available to weaker parties too, provided that this can be done without injury to the rights and duties of others or of the community itself (*The Church Today* § 78).

Under American law there is no recognition of the theory of the just war of self-defense except as it may be embodied in U. S. subscription to international treaties and organizations. The Constitution gives to the Federal Congress the right to wage war and raise armies without reference to the purpose of the war or the use of the armies. In spite of legal challenges, the courts have upheld the right of the government to compel military service of a man during a war which he believes to be an unjust war of aggression. American law does give recognition in different ways to the right of conscientious objection to war, but not to the right of a citizen to refuse participation in a particular war he believes to be unjust. Since the unjust war theory is commonly accepted by great numbers of American citizens, it must be questioned if its non-recognition by the law can be justified.

One case among many will illustrate the distinction. Captain Dale E. Noyd was a career officer in the United States Air Force. As a member of the military establishment, Captain Noyd clearly did not believe that all war was immoral. For twelve years Noyd served his country in diverse military capacities as a pilot and an instructor at the United States Air Force Academy. As American participation in the Vietnam war increased, Captain Noyd engaged in a lonely battle of conscience. He gradually came to the conviction that the American position in the war was immoral. Noyd then requested permission to resign his commission; this was refused. A request to be reclassified a conscientious objector within the military was refused on the grounds that Noyd did not believe all war was immoral (only this particular war). Noyd was then ordered to train pilots for duty in Vietnam. He refused. He was courtmartialed in March, 1968, and sentenced to a term at hard labor.

Almost a quarter of a century before Captain Noyd stood before American military judges, a group of German military and civil leaders were condemned to death by another group of American judges at Nuremberg. If Nuremberg represented growth in international morality, it was in the establishment of the proposition that there is such a thing as unjust war, and no individual has a right to participate in such a war. Many people widely hailed the Nuremberg trials as an infusion of a basic moral sense into the law which attempts to specify man's civic obligations. While the position of the State Department that war is legally justifiable as a prevention of external aggression against an ally is not unreasonable, Nuremberg clearly imposes on the American conscience the duty of allowing Captain Noyd to respect his conscience. In our treatment of Captain Noyd we not only violate the very principle we helped to incorporate into international law, we also outrage the right to conscience which we so piously proclaim. This is our failing, a failing comparable to that of the citizens of Nazi Germany.

There is serious reason to doubt that the just war theory of self-defense has any validity today. In the last few decades the United States has fought several major wars on the grounds that it was resisting unjustified aggression into the territory of allied quasi-nations such as the Republics of Korea or South Vietnam. To a great extent, the justification of these military actions required the recognition of unjustifiable ideological aggression by a Marxist philosophy against democratic structures. The failure of the American Congress to declare war in either the Korean or the Vietnam conflicts indicated serious doubts about the political, military and moral status of the American position in these conflicts. While the entrance of China into the Korean War made that conflict seem more like a conventional force-resisting-aggression use of military power, the participation of the United States in the

Vietnam conflict has produced serious moral doubts as to the justification for American involvement. While some Christian moralists label American activities as a "just war," and some lawyers believe that there is no violation of international law, many feel that neither morality nor law can justify wholesale destruction of portions of Vietnam by American troops under a theory that the United States is defending either itself or the Saigon government from aggression by other Vietnamese who supported a Marxist form of government.

The problem of Vietnam points up the difficulty of the unjust war theory in twentieth-century practice. As the world community undergoes dramatic changes because of increasing communications and universal fear of the use of nuclear and chemical warfare, the situations which can be identified as "unjust aggression" in the classical sense diminish. The words of Pope Paul to the United Nations on October 4, 1965, echo the feeling of many that *all* forms of war must disappear from the earth:

> the blood of millions of men, that numberless and unheard of sufferings, useless slaughter and frightful ruin, are the sanction of the part which unites you, with an oath which must change the future history of the world: No more war, war never again.

Perhaps military action can be justified when the ideological life of an allied community is in danger. Perhaps even the obliteration of a substantial physical part of the community one seeks to defend can be justified, but the Vietnam War forced on the conscience of both the Christian and the citizen the question: to what *extent* can I use force in self-defense. Most men would agree that any community, including a nation, has the right to defend itself against those who are attempting to destroy it. But can it morally and legally do so when the only way to defend is to destroy? Can one destroy a village to prevent the enemy from doing so? Can one destroy a community to prevent the acceptance of a political-social-economic ideology which the "defending" allied nation believes is wrong?

If so called "wars of national liberation" can be defeated only by intensive waging of guerrilla warfare which destroys vast numbers of lives, can such guerrilla warfare be justified? Inherent in these wars is the assumption that civilians must be killed in rather large numbers. Even if one doesn't consider a largely conscripted army to be "civilian," the Vietnam type of war involves the deaths of many more non-combatants than was ever imagined by the medieval theologians who evolved the "just war of self-defense" theory. The Bishops of Vatican II proclaimed acts of war aimed at indiscriminate destruction of cities or extensive areas of population to be "a crime against God and man himself." If this is so, one must ask: are there many practicable forms of military activity which can be morally employed in modern warfare? If a nation cannot defend itself by moral means, does it still retain a right of self-defense? If one can win a guerrilla war only by poisoning the crops in areas of enemy concentrations, bombing bridges in civilian areas, torturing prisoners or using heavy artillery against villages, can the nation justifiably wage such a war at all?

Nuclear, Chemical and Biological Weapons and a "Just" War

Another factor which has caused the self-defense theory of a just war to be questioned seriously is the development and build-up of nuclear and chemical weapons. The United States alone has a stockpile of chemical and biological weapons capable of destroying every living organism in the universe. Five nations possess quantities of nuclear weapons which could destroy vast populated areas. The use of chemical warfare is banned by international laws; nuclear test ban agreements limit signatory nations to certain forms of weapon testing. But the build-up of chemical and nuclear weapons continues. In the United States, at least, this build-up is justified on the basis of a deterrent to unjust aggression. In his papers on *The Justice of Deterrence* Paul Ramsey has defended the morality of deterrence. Without expressly condemning the deterrence theory of the arms race, the Bishops of the Second Vatican Council indicated their belief that stockpiling creates the causes of war:

> Whatever be the case with this method of deterrence, men should be convinced that the arms race in which so many countries are engaged is not a safe way to preserve a steady peace. Nor is the co-called balance resulting from this race a sure and authentic peace. Rather than being eliminated thereby, the causes of war threaten to grow gradually stronger (*The Church Today*, §81).

The conscience of the international community has formed a conviction that weapons which have an uncontrollable effect cannot be used. The rules drafted by the International Committee of the Red Cross in 1956 specify: "the use is prohibited of weapons whose harmful effect—resulting in particular from the dissemination of incendiary, chemical, bacteriological, radioactive or other agents—could spread to an unforeseen degree . . . from the control of those who employ them, thus endangering the civilian population." International law clearly prohibits the use of certain of these weapons. While international prohibitions of certain weapons have been in existence ever since the Second Lateran Council condemned the use of the crossbow in 1139, it was not until the twentieth century that the very survival of mankind came to depend on observance of these weapon prohibitions.

Hugo Grotius, the "father of international law," observed several centuries ago that nations commonly refrained from the use of poison as a weapon. But the chemical and biological weapons held by many modern states could produce more destruction than Grotius dreamed of. Chemical warfare is the use of toxic gases; biological warfare consists of using germs to create epidemics which destroy living organisms. Biological weapons are the most destructive and dangerous weapons ever designed by man since their effects are uncontrollable in both space and time. Chemical warfare, at least, is subject to more discriminatory uses. Although there were earlier treaties on the subject, the international legal basis for the prohibition of chemical and biological warfare is the Geneva Protocol of 1925. In the Protocol every major nation of the world except Japan and the United States agreed to accept the prohibition against "poisonous or other gases" and "bacteriological methods of warfare."

This agreement reflects the conscience of humanity. Is there any doubt but that it binds the nations which did not sign the Protocol? In 1947 the International Military Tribunal at Nuremberg proclaimed that "the law of war is to be found not only in treaties but in the customs and practices of states which gradually obtained universal recognition." That non-use of gas or germs has become the custom and practice of states is apparent from the fact that even a madman like Hitler did not employ them against the advancing allies although Germany had some of the most advanced chemical and biological weapons at that time.

No nation has ever used biological weapons. A few nations have used chemical weapons. In Vietnam American troops employed napalm. Napalm is an incendiary substance which has been used in the form of bombs dropped from planes, shot from "flame throwers," or placed as landmines. The burns caused by napalm are deep, usually third-degree. Terrible scars and deformities result from such burns. Death among those burned by napalm is not unusual with mortality among children running extremely high. In addition to burns, napalm frequently causes carbon monoxide poisoning, especially among those who attempt to take shelter in enclosed areas. There has been much effort to justify the use of napalm in Vietnam. The fact that so many civilians have been killed or deformed by napalm is dismissed as a "side-effect" of war. Some government spokesmen have attempted to justify American use of napalm by citing the horrors the Viet Cong have done to civilians. Even if one accepts the concept of a "just war," can the American conscience condone its violation of international law by the use of chemical warfare? One can legitimately question the use of napalm as a military weapon on the basis of our Vietnam experience.

The United States is the only nation which has used radioactive weapons in war. Unless one accepts the strained reasoning of some international lawyers as to the application of nineteenth century treaties, there is no clear prohibition on the use of nuclear weapons. There are treaties among the major powers which limit the right to test such weapons, and there are treaties which aim at preventing proliferation of the weapons. It may be that the conscience of the international community is developing a conviction that nuclear weaponry should be prohibited. The development of so called "clean" bombs does allow a discriminating use of nuclear weapons against purely military objectives, but the reluctance of any nation to use them may show a fear that once they are employed there may result an escalation to weapons of a more destructive type.

In light of the general agreement of men to the unlawfulness and immorality of chemical and biological weapons, and the growing distaste for nuclear weaponry, is there any longer justification for the stockpiling of such weapons? It is commonly thought that the possession of such weapons is a deterrence to unjust aggression or to the use of the weapons by an enemy. Perhaps the argument is tenable, but the warning given by the Bishops of the Second Vatican Council should give a fearful humanity pause to reconsider its conduct:

> Therefore, it must be said again: the arms race is an utterly treacherous trap for humanity, and one which injures the poor to an intolerable degree. It is much to be feared that if this race persists, it will eventually spawn all the lethal ruin whose path it is now making ready (*The Church Today* §81).

The Issue of Violent Civil Disobedience

When St. Paul wrote to the Christians of Rome in the year 58 A.D., he explained that they had a duty to obey the laws of the state:

> You must obey the governing authorities. Since all government comes from God . . . the state is there to serve God for

your benefit. If you break the law, however, you may well have fear: the bearing of the sword has its significance . . . You must obey, therefore, not only because you are afraid of being punished, but also for conscience' sake. (Rom. 13: 1–5).

The author of the First Letter of St. Peter advocates the same viewpoint:

> For the sake of the Lord, accept the authority of every social institution: the emperor, as the supreme authority, and the governors as commissioned by him to punish criminals and praise good citizenship. God wants you to be good citizens . . . Have respect for everyone and love for our community, fear God and honour the emperor. (1 Peter 2: 13–17).

Clearly the Jew or Christian should have a conscientious respect for civil authority. But the historical experience of man since the apostolic age has demonstrated that the conscience of the believer sometimes causes him to disobey the law. Is this justifiable?

Both moralists and lawyers use the term "civil disobedience" frequently today. The term has various meanings. One form of civil disobedience is *violent resistance* to the laws or even the existence of an illegally established government. Moralists have unanimously agreed that there is a moral right actively to resist the commands of a usurping civil authority; such is the case where a government establishes itself contrary to the constitution or fundamental law of the state. However, since lawyers are pragmatic men, they tend to support the right of a *de facto* government to be obeyed as long as its legislation is just and reasonable. On two occasions the United States Supreme Court has refused to rule against a usurping state government. In 1849, the Court refused to find that a government in Rhode Island holding power contrary to the state constitution was guilty of a trespass. Critical in this case was the fact that the President of the United States had treated the usurping government as the existing authority in the state. In 1900, the Court was asked to rule on a suit by a man named Taylor who had been certified as the lawfully elected Governor of Kentucky and had taken the oath of office. Taylor's opponents contested his election and eventually managed to usurp effective political power. The Supreme Court refused to help Taylor regain the office from which he was being unlawfully excluded. A court of law had no right to answer the "political" question of which government should rule Kentucky.

Moralists seem agreed that the rule of a usurping government can be resisted, but there seems little agreement on the right to resist unjust laws imposed by a legitimately established government. Many moralists follow Thomas Aquinas and argue that a tyrannical government is not ordered to the common good and may be overthrown by force. However, others, such as Werner Schöllgen, argue that tyrannicide is a vestige of heathenism which the Christian cannot accept. This position sees passive resistance or martyrdom as the only Christian alternative to the unjust rule of the tyrant. A contemporary example indicates how unresolved this question is. The philosophy of Camilo Torres, who gave up the active priesthood to support a violent revolution against an unjust governmental-ecclesiastical-social structure, has deeply divided the church in Latin America. The consternation over the activities of former Maryknoll religious such as Thomas and Marjorie Melville and John Hogan indicates that many Christians do not believe in social revolution. The Second Vatican Council left open the possibility of revolution but taught that the ultimate solution rests with the Christian's own conscience:

> Where public authority oversteps its competence and oppresses the people, these people should nevertheless obey to the extent that the objective common good demands. Still it is lawful for them to defend their own right and those of their fellow citizens against any abuse of this authority (*The Church Today*, § 74

The conduct of two sincere Catholic military officers toward the unjust activities of the Hitler regime points up the problems of conscience suffered by a Christian who lives under a tyrant. As the lack of justice in Germany became more apparent to him, a young member of the General Staff, Colonel Count Stauffenberg, determined that the only moral choice open to him was to kill Hitler and attempt to overthrow the Nazi regime. On July 20, 1944, Count Stauffenberg placed a bomb under a table being used by Hitler. Hitler was only injured and Stauffenberg and his fellow conspirators were killed. General Frido von Senger und Etterlin, "the defender of Cassino," was one of the most effective German field commanders in the Second World War. Von Senger, a former Rhodes scholar, was known for his moral revulsion to the techniques and goals of Hitler. Throughout the war Von Senger carried what he subsequently called "the burden of my conscience." He always obeyed that conscience and ignored any order which he considered immoral. By his passive resistance to the tyrant, Von Senger saved many innocent persons from unjust treatment. Who was the true Christian, Count Stauffenberg or General Von Senger? Were they both? Was neither?

Active or Passive Resistance to "Unjust" Laws

Thomas Aquinas taught that a human law which was lacking in right reason is no law at all. In *Pacem in Terris* Pope John XXIII wrote that a law which is contrary to the moral order cannot bind the conscience of the citizen since "obedience to God comes before obedience to man" (Acts 5:29). American law makes some provision for the right of a man to violate an unjust law. Long before the American Revolution the British government put a New York printer named John Peter Zenger on trial for printing some true statements about the political corruption of crown officials. British law did not recognize truth as a defense to political libel; Zenger's lawyer argued that he had a right to tell the truth. The judge ordered the jury to convict Zenger. The jury found him not guilty. Ever since that day a criminal lawyer has had a right to argue to the jury that his client has been charged with breaking an unjust law, and the jury has a right to return a finding of not-guilty even though the evidence shows beyond a reasonable doubt that the defendant did violate the law.

American jurisprudence recognizes the supremacy of society's judgment that a particular law is just over the judgment of the individual. In 1878, the United States Supreme Court affirmed the conviction of George Reynolds for bigamy. Reynolds was a member of the Church of the Latter Day Saints of Our Lord Jesus Christ, which advocated polygamy. Reynolds argued that the federal statute prohibiting polygamy was an unjust and unconstitutional infringement of a man's right to practice religion. The court ruled that Reynold's religious convictions did not empower him to violate the law. As to the prohibition of polygamy, the court cited the rejection of the practice throughout Western society. Chief Justice Waite wrote: "As a law of the organization of a society under the exclusive dominion of the United States, it [Congress] provided that plural marriage shall not be allowed. Can a man excuse his practices to the contrary because of his religious belief? To permit this would be to make the professed doctrines of religious belief superior to the law of the land, and in effect to permit every citizen to become a law unto himself. Government could exist only in name under such circumstances."[1]

That the individual has a right to disobey a positive law or order which he can demonstrate to be unjust may be accepted in some legal circles because of American participation in the Nuremberg trials of German war criminals. In 1967, a physician and army officer, Captain Howard Levy, was court-martialed for his refusal to train medics for service in Vietnam. Captain Levy argued that the order violated the medical code of ethics and that his obeying the order would mean his approval of the "illegal" activities of the medics in Vietnam. The law officer of the court hearing the charges ruled that Levy would be allowed to introduce evidence that American military forces in Vietnam were violating international law

---

[1] Reynolds v. U.S. 98 U.S. 145 (1878).

and morality. While Levy was convicted and sentenced to hard labor, the allowance of this defense was significant.

May an individual break a local law which he believes violates a more fundamental law? Moralists speak of the right to disobey a human law which violates the "natural law." American law predicates its answer not on the *belief* of the lawbreaker but on a *determination* that the local law does or does not in fact violate a superior law. In November, 1872, Susan B. Anthony voted in an election in Rochester, New York, in violation of a New York law prohibiting women from voting. In 1873, Miss Anthony's attorney argued that the New York law was contrary to the United States Constitution. The judge told the jury that the local law did not violate the Constitution and Miss Anthony was convicted. She could have appealed the judge's instruction, but the citizen's right to break an unjust law depends on its being actually unjust (i.e. in violation of the Constitution).

Civil Disobedience as a Social Protest

During the mid-sixties a number of Judeo-Christian theologians stated their approval of public protests against social injustices, even if the protest disrupted the public peace, constituted a trespass, or violated reasonable local laws. Other moralists approved boycotts, sit-ins and other forms of protest only if they were non-violent. Some writers, such as Paul Ramsey, argued that a sit-in was coercive and could be used only within the traditional context of a Christian's right to use force. In a nation with a history of dramatic social protest, from the Boston Tea Party to sit-ins at draft boards, there is much sympathy even with those who violate a reasonable and just law to call attention to some social deficiency. In recent years Americans have disrobed in public, thrown ashes at public officials, painted slogans on public buildings, violated injunctions against certain types of parades, taken control of buildings on college campuses, and stretched out across airport runways. In each of these cases, the demonstrators would have to admit that the prohibitory law was just. The gesture of a Philip Berrigan in pouring lamb's blood into Selective Service files is praised as a moral protest; the draft card burnings are cited as a desirable prod to the moral conscience of America. But the moralist adds a clause to their praises: he who violates a just law to promote a cause or protect an evil may act morally, but the state has a right to punish him for his conduct. I doubt if any theologian would dispute the moral right of the federal courts to sentence Father Berrigan to prison for his violation of the law.

In punishing those who engage in civil disobedience the government must take care to stay within the law itself. To protest the Vietnam War a group of Michigan college students blocked the entrance to a Selective Service office in Ann Arbor. When the student deferments of two demonstrators, Peter Wolff and Richard Short, were revoked, and they were reclassified I-A, there were protests from many citizens. The protests insisted that the draft could not legally be used as a punishment. Misuse of the Selective Service process against those who engage in civil disobedience is apparent from the drafting of Brother David Darst F.S.C. and Father David W. Connor after they turned in their draft cards as a protest against the Vietnam War.

On June 6, 1966, Sidney Street, a decorated war veteran, was listening to a radio news broadcast in New York City. When the newscaster announced that civil rights leader James Meredith had been shot while walking down a Mississippi highway, Street became angry. He took an American flag to a street corner and burned it. When a crowd gathered, Street told them "if they let that happen to Meredith we don't need an American flag." Street was arrested and convicted under a New York law which prohibits public mutilation of the flag. The highest court of New York affirmed Street's conviction, saying his conduct was "an act of incitement, literally and figuratively 'incendiary' and as fraught with danger to the public peace as if he had stood on the street corner shouting epithets at passing pedestrians. The state may legitimately curb such activities in the interest of preventing violence and maintaining public order."[2]

The forms of social protest which violate reasonable laws are unlimited. In New York a man was convicted of displaying offensive objects on the family clothesline as a protest against high property taxes. Citizens have had their bank accounts attached because they failed to pay a part of their income taxes which they felt would be used for military purposes. A Catholic woman marine was court-martialed for refusing to wear her uniform, a gesture she made in protest over the war in Vietnam. In 1966, the United States Supreme Court upheld the conviction of 31 persons who had been protesting the jailing of "political prisoners" by demonstrating on the grounds of a Florida jail. Two Catholic pacifists who protested the war in Vietnam by burning their draft cards were convicted in Federal Courts. These men may have acted morally, but the state has a right to punish them for their civil disobedience. Indeed, it is the willingness of the protestor to suffer the punishment of the law which gives his act its greatest moral meaning.

The state must be careful not to violate the constitutional and natural right of man to free speech in its punishment of those who engage in acts of protest which endanger the public peace or violate the law. In 1931, the United States Supreme Court reversed a conviction of a man who had violated a California law by displaying a red flag in public. In 1934, the Court reversed the conviction of Dirk De Jonge for addressing a public labor protest meeting in violation of an Oregon law against such meetings. In 1938 the Court reversed the conviction of a Jehovah's Witness, Alma Lovell, for distributing literature on a Griffen, Georgia, street without the permission of the city as required by an anti-litter ordinance. In 1963 the Supreme Court reversed the convictions of 187 Negroes who had been prosecuted for "breach of peace" when they sang the Star Spangled Banner and listened to a "religious

---

[2] People v. Street, 20 N.Y.S. 2d 491 (1967).

harangue" on the grounds of the South Carolina state house. In 1966, the Court reversed the breach of peace convictions of a group of Louisiana Negroes who sat quietly in a public library and refused to leave when requested to by the librarian. In each of these cases it might be argued that the state has a right to outlaw and punish conduct which will upset the peace and order. The state has such a power, but as these cases indicate it is subject to the limitation that the state may not prohibit man from exercising his fundamental rights. As explained by Justice Fortas:

> We are here dealing with an aspect of a basic constitutional right—freedom to petition the Government for a redress of grievances. As this court has repeatedly stated, these rights are not confined to verbal expression. They embrace appropriate types of action.[3]

The Fathers of the Second Vatican Council indicated that the dignity of man requires the state to extend to its subjects the "rights of free assembly, of common action, of expressing personal opinions, and of professing a religion both privately and publicly" (*The Church Today* § 73).

To maintain public order and still allow dissent is a great legal and moral challenge to free men.

---

[3] Brown v Louisianna 383 U.S. 131 (1966).

INDEX